FRAGMENTED COGNITION

The Scourge of Social Media

FRAGMENTED COGNITION

The Scourge of Social Media

Krishna Nath Pandey, Ph.D

Yesha Sikka, Research Assistant

ZORBA BOOKS

Published by Zorba Books, November 2021

Website: www.zorbabooks.com
Email: info@zorbabooks.com

Title :- Fragmented Cognition: The Scourge of Social Media

Print book ISBN :- 978-93-90640-55-3
Ebook ISBN :- 978-93-90640-40-9

Zorba Books Pvt. Ltd. (opc)
Sushant Arcade,
Next to Courtyard Marriot,
Sushant Lok 1, Gurgaon – 122009, India

Contents

Dedication

Mala Pandey (My Wife) who enacted 'beauty' and tolerated the author i.e. 'beast' of the fabled fairy tale.

Preface

Social media exposure to the humans starts since the birth itself though not directly perse. However, the direct exposure becomes ubiquitous with the inset of infancy. This continuum moves on and on with the onset of childhood and its progression across tween years, adolescence and teen years growing on to the threshold of adulthood. The mass media overpowers *homo sapiens* and the devil becomes the monster captivating the human beings in a 'virtual world 'leading to incapacitating the capabilities of the human brain itself. The mass media enabling the ageism manifests this strange human being to pass into the oblivion through the process of death. We love the virtual world and can spend hours living in it. Playing games, surfing on social media, watching movies, playing YouTube based videos are the Quality Times. Has the virtual world now become the new real world? Can we continue to live and behave as if the virtual world were the real world?

While social media have raised the profile of ordinary people to stardom and now you watch YouTube stars with robust standing and their fans following them are even ready to die for those stars. But the other side contains intense trolling and witch-hunt, if their followers and others disagree with the choices these people make and this may lead to negative psychological impact resulting in even extreme step such as committing suicide by these 'stars'.

'New technology' developments coupled with a changed lifestyle during the pandemic forced people to adopt new technologies and spend more time on the internet to enable them to work from a safe environment, usually a home. This encouraged a culture of work from anywhere and at anytime limiting the social interactions culminating to isolation, and increased focus on the screen.

For spreading awareness or disseminating the information, the social media are invaluable tools that have quick 'delivery' and has a low delivery cost. Sometimes, it is difficult to distinguish between real news and the fake news. Social media delivery of news is quick almost at the speed of light. This poses a real danger if 'fake news' is taken as real news and the same spreads like a wildfire. Cyberloafing is killing the valuable time. Privacy is getting abused and it is leading to addiction compelling people to live in a *virtual world*. The trolling of a celebrity for a statement is very prevalent. Spoiling the reputation of the 'Real' leaders which is now the norm rather than an occasional occurrence. A smart algorithm used by the master may make him the controller of power, pelf and prosperity instantly.

Though there is a widespread belief that social media impact cognitive skills. The jury is still out whether the impact is 'real' and if so what kind of impact it has? Will social media lower the cognitive skills or sharpen them? If cognitive skills are impacting them then which cognitive skills are impacted. This needs serious deliberations.

If social media have such wide-ranging ramifications on our well being and life, it is a must that we examine it closely forthwith so that we can help enhance people's lives by throwing light on the benefits and harmful effects of social media. How young can be helped to harness social media to their benefit and limit its negative impact. This book may be useful in this domain.

Acknowledgment

Ananya Ganesh (my PRANU) motivates me to keep writing as I want to be a 'noted' grandpa before I pass to the oblivion. My wonderful daughters, Neha and Medha love me very much as their PAPA. My Wife Mala stands my tantrums and mood swings. All of them want me to do 'something meaningful'. Thanks to all these persons.

My Son- in -law Ganesh Krishnamurthy always helps me in updating my articulation to become a techno-savvy individual. I love you Ganesh as your 'father'.

The help, protection and performing the job of a gabien was available from my elder brothers, late Sankata Prasad Pandey, Vishwanath Pandey and Sona Bhabhi, accept my PRANAM in your heavenly abode. My eldest sister-in law Raghumati converted me into her 'everything'. Thanks Bhabhi.

My elder brother Vashista Muni Pandey and Malati Bhabhi gave me money, support and warmth of security. A huge 'Thank you to this 'great couple'.

My elder borther Narad Muni Pandey used to be a friend more than a brother. Thanks DADA. Satyabhama Bhabhi turned out to be a 'negative motivator' Thank you for inspiring me !

The role played by Kamala Sahani, my foster mother, B. K Banerjee Sahib ; the mentor for my indoctrination into a C -Suite executive and my Ph. D Supervisor, Prof. Sreelatha (Director, SOMS, IGNOU) has been invaluable. Thanks to all of you from the core of my heart for making me 'someone'.

Yesha Sikka has got her place on the front and back cover pages for her immense and untiring support.

The team of Zorba Books is rocking in whatever task assigned to it . Kudos!

Introduction

The 21st century has seen the dawn of 'over-information', virtual reality; online learning and free fall of all sorts of quickest metamorphosis in the realm of main stream of globalized world.

Naturally, the internet went beyond the control of an individual, institution or entity. This paved the way for the critically important cyber – security, rarity of the novel algorithm, artificial intelligence and machine learning. Such a scenario has flooded the cyber -space for every *Tom, Dick and Harry*. Chaotic freedom to all those who could lay their hands on the smartphone may write whatever they want, picturize, shoot and upload almost anything and everything as it is on the social media platforms. The ubiquitous platform, commonly known as social media has disrupted almost all the norms of societal and the behavioral patterns thereof.

The impact of this has established 'work anytime from anywhere' and tag any individual present in any part of the world. This has led to the encroachment on individual and personal freedom besides the ease. It has created a 'dent in the universe' in the words of Steve Jobs. This has compelled us to look at it from the situation in the aftermath of the use of omnipresent social media.

Chapter I

INTRODUCTION

- Social media- which is a product of digital technology has taken over our society initially as *third industrial revolution* and more recently as fourth one as well.
- Creative Writing in English- is an art or subject matter of English literature as academic curriculum. Without going into technicalities of what are constituents of creative writing, I shall like to define it in most basic manner. "Creative writing" has two words "creative" and "writing". "Creative" in respect of person, as per Collins dictionary is defined as "A creative person has the ability to invent and develop original ideas, especially in the arts". If these ideas are put in writing, it becomes creative writing. In literature examples are –Poetry, Plays, Movie and Television scripts, Fiction (novels, novellas, and short stories), Songs etc. Therefore any writing that is original expression is cretive writing
- Critique- as per Collins dictionary means "a critical analysis or evaluation of a subject, situation, literary work, etc"

A lot has been written, discussed, spoken about creative writing in English as subject matter of English literature. With the invention of the written word, we started writing stories. This is where the history of creative writing really begins. Notwithstanding these eras in English language, narrative has been dominantly in textural realm.

However, with the advent of digital technologies, narrative on creative writing is going through a paradigm shift.

This shift is nothing short of revolution and though it has become a reality yet it is still not on the radars of academia as a discipline. A discipline which integrates English literature to digital technology.

This book attempts to explore impact of this integration as it is happening.

The third industrial revolution called the digital revolution began in the 1960s. It was ushered in by the development of semiconductors, mainframe and personal computing, the internet and other digital technologies. Today we are treading along with fourth industrial revolution. Klaus Schwab, a professor who founded the World Economic floated this terminology "the fourth industrial revolution". Building on the digital revolution, "the fourth industrial revolution" plunged into existence along with this century.

"The fourth industrial revolution, however, is not only about smart and connected machines and systems. Its scope is much wider. Occurring simultaneously are waves of further breakthroughs in areas ranging from gene sequencing to nanotechnology, from renewables to quantum computing. It is the fusion of these technologies and their interaction across the physical, digital and biological domains that make the fourth industrial revolution fundamentally different from previous revolutions."

A byproduct of this development has been the introduction and subsequent rise of Social Media platforms. These platforms are particularly popular among young adults, who are their significant users Social media is defined variously in literature (Mahadi et. al, 472). Some researchers call it "socially interactive technologies," for example instant messaging or text messaging or other networks which offer past-paced, inexpensive online communication which allows social interaction to start and evolve (Bryan et. al, 2006).

It can be defined as "the relationship that exist between network of people," (Walter& Riviera, 2004). While Merriam Webster explains it as "forms of electronic communication (such as websites for social networking and microblogging) through which users create online communities to share information, ideas, personal messages, and other content (such as videos)."

The result of these advancements is that people across ages are constantly using these to connect, express their feelings and publish their creative content. Some of the social media Platforms being used these days are listed below.

- Facebook
- Twitter
- Instagram
- Goodreads
- Pinterest
- WordKrowd
- WritersCafe.org
- Wattpad
- Commaful

One of the areas going through of tremendous evolution due to technology is human language. Research is now being conducted on how technological advances are transforming languages, specifically English. And I take up English since this is the most preferred language of communication [or the most widely used 'link-language'] across the world). In fact, as per Statista. com, the leading online source of stats, as of January 2020, English was the most popular language online, representing 25. 9 percent of worldwide internet users.

If we put together "social media" and "English Language," we see a new amalgamation creating new forms of language and Creative Writing. This is because with the rising popularity of social media platforms including but not limited to – Facebook, Instagram, Twitter, and blogging sites – everyone has become an aspiring author, willing to put forth their creation for the world to read. Add to this the reality that today people create and consume content at an unprecedented pace, and communication also happens at a speed unheard of before - All this has resulted in the English being transformed to 'fit' the new communication needs.

We see changes in two areas, the way the language is transforming and second, and most relevant to our context, the reinvention of Creative Writing.

Over the decades, Creative Writing has come to be defined by the stalwarts of language and literature in a particular way. This definition includes the language as it is written in its standard form and the structure of the sentence of that language. The research discussing Creative Writing often covers the process of how to develop creative writing skills but not what constitutes good writing. Current research focuses on creative writing in schools and academia, but not the craft itself and its evolution.

This entails collating the entirety of the parameters gaining the consciousness on the way to become a 'classic. ' That is often relegated to the realm of feelings of the reader.

We attempt to take a look at some of the concerns and changes in language and creative writing apropos these developments and what we can do about it.

The use of social media for creative writing and internet started somewhere in the middle of last decade of nineteenth, we will trace back to the first definition of creative writing. We will need to begin at the beginning – to the earliest times when creative writing was recognized as a literary form. From there we will attempt to understand the influences that impact the creator and the language he or she uses to 'create' the work of written art. Can any and every piece of work whether using standard English language as we know it, or the modern urban dictionary that has come to include all sorts of deviations and appropriations of language be called creative writing? And what impact does digitization have on it?

We will also attempt to see what impact do gatekeepers of quality – editors – have on creative writing and what happens when they are removed from the equation of publishing a piece of creative writing. All this leading into the digital age we are in wherein the very act of 'creation' has undergone a metamorphosis and the definition of being a 'published' 'author' has changed.

Today, storytelling comes in different formats - we have mobile storytelling; storytelling on apps; twitter, Facebook; blogs and self-publishing.

New terms are being introduced in language to convey what exists today. So what is creative writing in the new era? How is technological revolution re-defining creative writing and the impact it has on the language itself? And what are the effects of platforms on writing.

This researcher is aware of some of the diluting factors in standard written English being a being a content marketer, and creative writer; who has also witnessed some written pieces which are really bad work and are available online as well as the accessibility to budding authors that digitization has brought about. This is what has motivated this researcher to undertake this study for this research work.

Aims and objectives of this Research

1. Current research focuses on teaching of creative writing but not the craft itself and to study the evolution of Creative writing over the years.
2. To study the factor of evolution and review the past writings of this genre to find out the patterns for emulation of future writers. Analyzing the changing or developing features of creative writing by looking at the writings of authors from Aristotle to current times i. e., 2020.
3. To analyze the changing and developing features of creative writing from the past till now.
4. To understand how the socio-economic-political and developments of the current era as well as the previous one of lack of information and its influence on the authors – i. e., prior to the advent of social media platforms (1995). Also, for the current era to deduce how platforms of publishing influence the language and writing itself in the context of Natural Language Processing.
5. To trace the impact of technological advancements on creative writing in English.

Hypothesis

Digitization and the Fourth Industrial Revolutionrevolution and the rise of Social Media Platforms are transforming the English language landscape rapidly. In their wake there have been unprecedented changes in the English Language and Creative Writing per se. With everyone and anyone becoming an author by publishing their work online, there is a greater need to build a framework replicating that of the gatekeepers of the past, namely, Editors, to ensure the sanctity of the language is retained while giving wings to new creative forms of writing. With advancements in digital publishing, now a novel, is no longer unidimensional but incorporates other media – songs, images, etc. It also no longer follows a linear narrative. In fact, fiction on Twitter is gaining popularity, a platform that does not give itself to linearity. In such a case we see a dawn of a new form of Creative fiction that not only includes these new formats but new languages as well.

Human beings are as much a product of the environment as they are creators of it. New terms are being introduced in language to convey what exists today. Today, storytelling is being done on various formats – on mobile phones and on apps like Twitter, Facebook, Instagram; blogs and even self-publishing platforms like Amazon.

Digitization is available to an increasing amount of people from various social backgrounds.

Anyone and everyone has become a writer and author, in most cases becoming self-editors. So how do we define creative writing in the new era? How is technological revolution re-defining creative writing and the impact it has on the language itself? And is there a way to manage the quality of writing that is being introduced almost daily into the digital world?

Over the years, evolution in creative writing has enriched literature with a new voice, representing the coming of age of a generation that saw the advent of Internet and the myriad platforms. In today's times, digital tools affect writing in significant ways including broadening the audience for authors and encouraging collaboration. Online platforms allow writers to work alongside and edit each other's work resulting in instant peer review.

On the flip side, however, there is an increasing danger of informality creeping into creating writing standards. Add to this the incapacity of today's "quick authors" to navigate complicated texts, and handle copyright and issues related with the use of intellectual capital in their compositions.

Scope and limitations

The existing research on creative writing focuses on the craft as it is being taught in the schools and academia, but not the craft itself and its evolution. Though there are some papers that have started to address the issue, there is a gap in this genre.

The impact of Social media platforms on creative writing is a relatively new topic and hence, the research available on this is scarce. There are researchers who are now writing about the trends in English language as well as the popularity of fiction on platforms such as Twitter, but it is all still in a nascent stage.

I have tried to research and read the current research as available online and even those being reported in new media, since that is where most of the questions are being raised. Being a comparatively novel topic, there is not much to go on, but I have tried to connect various diverse ideas, on whom research is available and to supplement by hypothesis.

It is a rapidly developing field, and I am sure, even as I write, new developments would have taken place.

Present significance of the Topic

The social media platforms and the evolution in language and Creative writing is here to stay. Infact, the next level of development in this area would be the introduction of AI and its use in creating content. Narrative Science is a technology company based in Chicago, Illinois that specializes in data storytelling.

Narrative Science is the leader in automated narrative generation for the enterprise. Powered by artificial intelligence, its Quill™ platform analyzes data from disparate sources, understands what is important to the end user and then automatically generates perfectly written narratives to convey meaning from the data for any intended consumer or business audience, at unlimited scale

My research in no way offers all solutions and ideas, but it is my hope it will be provide a platform on which future linguist and literature researchers will build upon.

So far research on these trends have been conducted by multinationals who have used the services of leading linguists to capitalize or understand this new phenomenon. This area of research would be useful for both English researchers as well as digital marketers and social media content strategists and new age digital publishers to understand the impact of technology on language and what the new generation is conversing and writing in.

Research Methodology

Qualitative research method will be adopted through exploratory and descriptive tools for understanding the texts in their socio-political context, their individual and comparative analysis, changing trends, relating the theory with the Creative Writing.

Chapter Breakup

Chapter 1: Introduction – About the thesis, approach and Methodology

Chapter 2: Discusses about what is creative writing. With introduction of digital media and social media platform how there is change in narrative. What was narrative style before digital transformation?

Chapter 3: In this chapter development of technology leading to the creation of social media platforms is discussed. The contribution mobile technology like smartphones, speed of transfer of data all contributing to popularity of such platform and also affordability of such platforms to masses. Advent of the Internet and Social Media platforms and their impact on creative writing and English language is analyzed Chapter 4: The Paradigm Shift – Author present and past; what is a classic. This chapter explores the views of different critics and authors in an effort to establish criteria of defining classic. This chapter also explores whether certain category of creative narratives on digital media can at all meet some of these criteria.

Chapter 5: Criteria and Benchmark of Creative Writing – Gatekeeping in the new era. This chapter examines consequences and remedies for absence of traditional filters of traditional gate keeping and can we create a framework?

Chapter 6: Conclusion

Chapter II

EVOLUTION OF COGNITION FOR CREATION

(Pre and Post Digital Era)

Overview

All this leading into the digital age we are in wherein the very act of 'creation' has undergone a metamorphosis and the definition of being a 'published' 'author' has changed.

The Internet has long history of evaluation, which has been discussed in chapter-3. The development of World Wide Web by a British scientist Tim Berner at CERN and its availability to public in 1991 was a ground breaking concept which laid the foundation of present day advent of digital age. The development by Tim Berner was followed by other technologies to make it available to public for creative writing. The emergence of technologies known as Web 2. 0 in the late nineties has enabled users to upload and manipulate content with remarkable ease. The treatise on digital technology revolutionizing the use of internet for creative writing has also been dealt in chapter-3. The origin of internet for our purpose can be placed around mid-nineties of 19th century

Let us trace back, first the definition of creative writing before origin of digital platforms and go on to see its evolution in post digital era.

2.1 Human beings are as much a product of the environment as they are creators of it.

Today, storytelling comes in different formats - we have mobile storytelling; storytelling on apps; twitter, Facebook; blogs and self-publishing.

New terms are being introduced in language to convey what exists today. So what is creative writing in the new era? How is technological revolution re-defining creative writing and the impact it has on the language itself?

And what are the effects of platforms on writing. Current research focuses on creative writing in schools and academia, but not the craft itself and its evolution.

What is creative writing? We can understand it as an act of creating a written work that is original and can be in various forms.

Over the decades, going back to the times of Aristotle we can find a mention of something akin to creative writing. If we delve into the research done in this area, we find that it was really a phrase that came into existence, somewhere between the first two world wars in American schools. It was used to distinguish writing that was not freshman English or report writing by Engineers (Wallace, 100)

Creative Writing is an act of imagination. Wallace calls it imaginative writing; writing as an art (Wallace, 100). In fact, he elaborates that this kind of writing has got nothing to do with information or routine form of communication "though it uses the same skills."

Research in this area has mostly focused on creative writing as taught in schools and universities and what the various processes involved. However, for the purposes of our paper and to understand the context in which Creative Writing has been understood historically, we take a look at what the stalwarts are saying about it. And from there we move on to researchers like Graeme Harper who talk about the future of creative writing in the digital space and the technological era that we are living in. I also take the liberty of expanding this definition to other forms of literature such as novels, classics and "Twitter Fiction," because after all what is taught is to make these creations. So basically bring them out of the classrooms to the real world.

To understand creative writing we need to go back to the beginning – to the earliest times when creative writing was recognized as a literary form. From there we will attempt to understand the influences that impact the creator and the language he or she uses to 'create' the work of written art. Can any and every piece of work whether using standard English language as we know it or the modern urban dictionary that has come to include all sorts of deviations and appropriations of language be called creative writing? And what impact does digitization have on it?

2.2 Definition of creative writing

As I mentioned earlier, for me creative writing could be defined as an act of creating a written work that is original and can be in various forms – a poem or a story or play.

In his book, The Future of Creative Writing, Graeme Harper writes, "Creative writing involves both the use of language and contributions to language. As a medium largely dependent upon written language, and with a complex and ever-changing relationship with spoken language too, even at the level of words being placed on a page (whatever kind of "page" that might be: paper, electronic, other), creative writing is heavily impacted upon by language change."

Creative writing is anything that goes beyond professional, journalistic, academic or technical forms of literature. It is an expression of human creativity and is an expression of an individual's experience. As language evolves, it not only impacts creative writing, but writers also influence the evolution of language. With the introduction of various platforms recently, the meaning of creative writing has changed according to where it is being featured. Likes Harper says above, a simple term like 'page' has come to mean different things. In the same way today we see stories being written in as little as 26 characters on Twitter, to messages in mobile apps, to blogs. Even publishing has come to mean as different things – from being featured in a blog, to be printed in a book, to being self-published or having an e-book. So has the term "creative writing" as we have understood so far traditionally has had to evolve?

In the times of the Ancient Greeks, creative writing as we understand today, did not really exist. However, literary criticism was very much alive since they had plays and poetry. Plato, Socrates and Aristotle were the main triumvirate of philosophy and literature in ancient Greek. However, though Plato criticised art in Book X of his Republic, Aristotle's Poetics can be seen as a response to the former. In it Aristotle discusses, Greek tragedy and poetry taking Homer's example. Poetics has had a major influence on literary theory.2

2.3 Plato and Aristotle – Beginnings of Literary Criticism

For Plato Ideas are the "origin and the underlying structure of the materialistic world." Plato's Ion is the first extant work on the theory of Literature in Western tradition. It is a very short dialogue between Socrates and Ion who is a rhapsode. Plato's view of Literature is on the whole negative. The other major view is that of Aristotle. Though he criticised poetry and literature as a form of imitation, he was not completely against it. For Plato philosophy was the basis of everything, however, for Aristotle, established poetry's independence from philosophy. 4 Plato and the Greek world, identified art as merely representational and hence misleading.

However, Aristotle was fascinated by the intellectual challenge of forming coherent systems and approached literature as a natural scientist. It is important to understand how literature and its creation have been viewed through the ages to get an accurate grasp of the changes happening now.

If we go through the literature present today on creative writing, we find that it is restricted to classroom teaching of writing. However, the process of creation of a piece of written work has more to it than just learning techniques. One of the biggest examples of how the definition of creative writing has changed is evident from the winners of the coveted Nobel Prize.

In 2016, in a major break from tradition, Bob Dylan, singer-songwriter, author and visual artist who has already many awards to his name was felicitated with this highest honor -Nobel Prize for Literature, for "having created new poetic expressions within the great American song tradition." Mr. Dylan, was the first musician to win the award for literature, and his selection was almost radical. In choosing a popular musician for the literary world's highest honor, the Swedish Academy, actually rewrote the definition of literature, creating a discussion as to whether song lyrics have the same literature value as poetry or novels. That begets the question, is the definition of creative writing expanding? Before going on to explore the new narrative styles that have arisen due to technological evolution, let us first try and understand the genesis of Creative Writing itself.

2.4 Historical evolution of Creative Writing

In mapping the rise of creative writing, D. G. Meyers in his insightful paper observes that the birth of this genre is a bit shrouded in mystery. There are many theories laid out for the same and he takes a look at those. To give an instance of how confusing the origins of creative writing are he quotes poet Dave Smith (Meyers, 278): "its pedigree is overlooked frequently but nevertheless exists from the pre-Socratic philosophers to the Scribler Club [sic] of Swift, Pope, Gay, etc. to Ransom, Warren, Tate, and other Fugitives, to the Harlem Renaissance, to the Beats, to Black Mountain, and unto university programs in creative writing." He comments that this description is faulty and is repeated by others like Stephen Wilber in his works, where he also attributes the emergence of creative writing to writer's workshops which flourished in Iowa from the early 1890s to the second decade of the twentieth century (Meyers, 278). Instead Meyers argues that "Creative Writing was devised as an explicit solution to an explicit problem. It has a clear beginning that can be clearly dated. ... it arose during a 60-year period from about 1880 to 1940 as an effort to reform the study of literature." (Meyers, ibid). He observes that creative writing is the name given to any effort that tries to restore the idea of "literature as an integrated discipline of thought and activity" (Meyers, 279). Though others have argued that creative writing always existed in the English speaking world, going back to 400 years (Meyers, Ibid), the fact is in the past it was a means of education to help students become complete persons through the writing of verse or poetry but not for the sake of becoming poets. In its evolution from that it lost its humanistic touch and turned into a means of becoming a writer and not all-rounded human being.

In fact the advanced study of literature in the late-19th century, especially in America, was dominated by German philologists (Meyers, ibid), which resulted in extreme focus on precision, uniformity and system rather than the humanistic ideals (Meyers, 281).

It is interesting to read through this because it has a great bearing on how Creative Writing came to be understood and judged over the decades. Instead of a means to become a better human and to reflect the human condition, it began to focus more on hard facts; instead of understanding the process of creation or why one writer was better than the other. (Meyers, ibid)

It was to bridge the gap that English literature had developed divorcing the how from creative writing that it started to emerge as a discipline of study. One of the earlier proponents of creative writing was Barette Wendell (1855-1921), he used the term creative writer for himself to distinguish himself from other writers. By this time creative writing had also started to exclusively come to mean fiction because the philological era dissociated it from non-fiction. (Ibid, 284).

He was the one according to Meyer who completely revamped the teaching of creative writing, then known as English Composition.

It is in this essay that for the first time we come across a mention of what makes a good piece of writing so. Meyers observes that "Wendell's own experience of writing for publication had convinced him that good writing was "agreeable, as distinguished from correct," and that real writers felt themselves to be 'living in a real world as distinguished from a world of book. '" (Ibid, 284-85). He was opposed to the way English compositions had given birth to scholars who could be found "burrowing in detail until he cares mostly for technical exactitude."

What becomes clear from this is that creative writing in its earliest form was a way to help students become better human beings. It was a means of self-discovery. Somewhere in between, when it was overtaken by philologists, it entered the realm of correctness and consistency. However, since it always was a means to help people express their personal experience, something Wendell also emphasized, in the language closest to them, it found its way back to expression and away from technicalities. Under his influence, instruction in writing became distinct from study of texts, or the exhaustive analysis that makes up the text (Ibid, 287). For him, "the object... was to produce something not unlike literature – but by literature was meant descriptive writing full of sensory detail, which did not preclude the writing of poems and stories. Yet the innovation of accepting poems and stories was institutionalized by the doctrine of deliberate cultivation of personal experience; and it was the substance (personal experience) and not the form (poems and stories) that was of first importance." (Ibid, 286)

Creative Writing under its own name was first taught by Hughes Mearns (Ibid, 288). He replaced English with Creative writing wherever he taught and emphasized that English came out of student's everyday lives and was not something relegated to academics and theory alone. For him students of literature had to be "makes of literature," and that they learned by continuously developing themselves. Under him students sought out their own reading, reaching out to contemporary authors rather than the classics whom he scorned. This was perhaps the first time that a precursor to opening up the literary canon was observed (Ibid, 290). This is crucial for our discussion, since it identifies that even in the past Creative Writing and its proponents, always broke through the jaded confines of literature and classics or for that matter the accuracy of the language and pushed for self-expression, and encompassing the new literature. Meyers rightly observes that "it is more accurate to say that under creative writing a principle of usefulness or sustainability – a twist on the notion of decorum- replaces that of canonicity." (ibid, 290). Mearns was the first one to introduce "creative reading," in which he encouraged his students in literary study to not just read good poems but to write them and in that way learn what is good. He aimed to create art as a living thing.

In a way this has a bearing on our own reflection of what truly makes a good writing. Only when we read a variety of literature, question and then write, we are able to understand what is good.

From here creative writing under a new phase under Norman Foerster, who is credited for introducing this as a clear discipline in universities starting from IOWA. However, he categorically combined creative writing with criticism, since he felt both were important for a correct and thorough study of literature. (Meyers, 293). Foerster intended creative writing to be a separate study, like a workshop, "assisting all students of literature toward an inner comprehension of the art." (ibid).

The biggest difference between Foerster and Mearns' approach was that the former abhorred all types of creative self-expression. For him learning to write was not just about expressing oneself but also "learning to assimilate and make use of cultural values implicit within the forms of writing." (Ibid)

Another perspective about Creative Writing is presented by Wallace Stegner that I shared in the beginning of this chapter. He talks about another aspect of this kind of writing that leads us what actually makes creative writing and how it differentiates from other forms of writing.

2.5 Components of creative writing

Impact of socio-political and now technological advances on writers

Going back to our discussion, creative writing has two main components – the language its written in and the skill of the author or "imagination" as wc called it and its ability to affect the reader. I say affect and not influence because each individual who reads a piece of fiction or creative work develops a very personal relationship with it.

Thus, the discussion on creative writing encompasses both the creation and the act of creating it. An author is not distinct from the society that he lives and breathes in. Even if he or she creates a piece of fiction, somewhere it is affected by the times the author exists. Of course, in the past, there have been thinkers who have imagined a world not yet existing and brought new worlds into being. This is evident if one reads science fiction or even works of philosophical discourse. For example, if we look at Les Misérables we see how Victor Hugo reflects society of that time and even talks of the Battle of Waterloo. Similarly, if we look at Pride and Prejudice we get to understand the realities of the women in those times. The language that the authors use, as well as the format they write in is indicative of the era they live. We have also seen the impact that evolution in technology has on writing. Take for instance the times of writing from an ink pen, to a typewriter to the computers of today.

The question that arises at this point is that does a change in technology have an impact on the author? After all isn't writing confined to the realm of imagination? And does this change Creative Writing. Apparently it does.

2.6 Creative Writing in the 21st Century

In his work Re(Writing) Craft Mayers argues against the institutional conventional wisdom that the process of composing cannot be studied and is in fact is a process so intrinsic, individual or even mysterious that it cannot be analyzed. He in fact argues in favor of understanding of craft that moves away from "manipulation of the surface features of text" and towards the "process of generating a text." Taking into account the ideological, material, cultural and political forces that surround it. (Koehler, 381). He calls this craft criticism, a form of criticism that brings to the fore the production of text while relegating to the background the interpretation of text. As Koehler observes: "While literary criticism uses methods of interpretation to examine the ways imaginative literature operates, craft criticism uses methods of production to examine the ways imaginative literature operates-and how it can help its authors and audience members engage critically with the cultural environment that surrounds them." (Ibid, 382)

What Mayers does is position craft criticism according to four basic categories – process, genre, authorship and institutionality. Koehler makes an important point regarding these four. According to him all of these intersect with digital technologies is one way or the other. I would like to quote him here since it is relevant for our discussion. Talking about how each of these categories can be examined in the context of digital technologies he says:

"Process: can a writer determine what a piece of writing will look like as it develops across digital technologies? What happens when poems intersect with songs, video and image while integrating reader response? Genre: Are blogs creative nonfiction? Authorship: how have notions of 'originality' changed in an open-source culture? Institutionality: how can scholars in creative writing help parse out and understand the shifting dynamics of print and electronic reading/writing practices as they are presently evolving in the academy at the undergraduate workshop level as well as the thesis for PHD and teacher training level?"

He observes how these four criteria will help us better understand the impact technological and contextual developments have on the process of creative production. (Koehler, 383)

If we take into account the first three criteria (process, genre, authorship), we come to see that digital technologies can and have brought about a change in the way authors produce text. In fact, they are transforming the literary landscape by redefining genres, language and composition itself.

However, to truly understand the effect technology has had on literary text we need to go to the beginning. In Koehler's essay he traces the evolution of digital processes and text by tracing the evolution of Hypertext (Hypertext is text which contains links to other texts. The term was coined by Ted Nelson around 1965). (2)He talks of the Kairos which in 1998 published a special issue on hypertext poetry and fiction. For the first time we are exposed to the concerns raised due to the "electronic threading of multiple narratives and themes in short stories, novels, and poetry made possible by hypertext." (Ibid, 383) With Hypertext was introduced the non-linearity of text due to its repetitive nature as well as the ability to visualize so one could read and see at the same time. In the nonlinear text the readers do not have to go through the text sequentially to read the text. This type of text has multiple reading paths. The readers decide the sequence of reading, not the author of the text. In a few years though it gave way to New Media which afforded multimodality. (Ibid.) The digital technologies provide opportunities for various modes of expression known as multimodality that can include digital text, images, gestures, sound, and movement. These modes can be used individually or in various combinations.

We had reached a stage in evolution of creative writing where the text was now exposed to a variety of media. Koehler quotes Jeff Rice and his The Rhetoric of Cool to underscore the point that rhetorical invention emerges out of a myriad influence (Rice, 10). And the same is the case with imaginative invention as per Koehler.

What we can infer from these arguments is the fact that an author is not isolated from the epoch he/she lives in. And creative writing studies being conducted to take into account the technological advancements. Now, a writer had more ways than one, simultaneously to present his/her story. This could include animated text, introduction of media – visual and audio to augment the story, etc. And so a new form of creative writing had emerged fueled by digital technologies.

This was also the time when boundaries around poetry, fiction and creative non-fiction were being redefined. Through Koehler's and Mayeres work we can now see how text changes across emergent technologies through the process category of digital craft criticism.

An area that has also seen significant change is the way books are published. From paper to e-books to pdfs to novels with multimedia – books have evolved a lot over the years. A pioneering work tracing this evolution is Katherine Hayles' Writing Machines. As it explains in its blurb it is a "pseudo-autobiographical exploration of the artistic and cultural impact of the transformation of the print book to its electronic incarnations." She delves in depth on three novels - TalanMemmott's trailblazing work Lexia to Perplexia, Mark Z. Danielewski's cult House of Leaves, and Tom Phillips's A Humument. Through her research we find out the treatment given to Danielewski's House of Leaves the way the novel borrows a visual template from digital writing but also the word House appears its in a blue ink as if hypertexted. The novel is accompanied by an album by Poe who loosely references the novel while the latter does the same for certain songs and lyrics. (Ibid, 385) This example shows how one piece of fiction can engage with different media creating a hybrid novel in the process. We can now experience texts across various media platforms. Koehler takes another example called Inanimate Alice and emphasizes that in the new age the relationship an author shares with his readers is as much dependant on the new media that help toestablishs it.

2.7 Digitization of Creative Writing and New Literature

Next Koehler examines how digitization has matured literature in the digital age and what has it come to mean for the digital natives.

To begin with it has been observed that digitization has forced open the tight-knit categorization of literature and its genres. In his essay Koehler cites certain examples to explain this phenomena.

He takes on Ander Monson's book Vanishing Point: Not a Memoir, which according to him stands at the intersection of memoir and creative non-fiction. The digital technologies at his disposal allow him to transform a memoir into what Koehler calls "Not a memoir." (Koehler, 387) The reason he does so is that Monson litters his memoir with "dagger like footnotes," that not just contain a text but can be in the form of a video, images or evolving text. This allows the author to move away from just talking about himself – the essence of a memoir – and introduce other topics completely non-related to him but for the reader to explore in case he wants to know more. Something that is very much prevalent today in the times of Google, where bloggers can introduced hyperlinks to other topics in case their reader want to know more. This allows him flexibility with the "genre of a memoir," thus breaking the confines of how it is understood to be traditionally.

In fact, in the book Monson had included an essay that he had also published on his website. It was later picked up for print in a magazine. Koehler points out that in the process of changing the piece from a digital to a traditional print platform, it actually underwent a change to affirm to the print format. In point of fact, conforming to the print genre actually changed its meaning. Though print as a medium will always be available to the Creative Writer, Koehler makes an important point:

"In this way, we will always be able to identify genres as they as they emerge and reconfigure across developing technologies, however a digital understanding of the genre prong of the craft criticism allows us a point of entry regarding the quality and nature of the interactions of those technologies on the conventions of the texts they product." (Koehler, 388)

In examining how the conventional genres are being changed due to digitization and rise of the Internet, Koehler also takes the example of the first Twitter novel, something that we also discuss in a different context later in the thesis. However, in his view, when authors like Rick Moody experimented on Twitter to write a novel, they defined their new work in terms of existing categories of genres. Though Twitter format (term later explained in this chapter) is nothing like any of the existing ones, instead of creating a new term for it, they described it, and the readers related to it, in terms they already knew. That is "they recruited other genres to help understand the modifications of the genre that surfaced" (Koehler, 389). For instance, when Moody descried his work to a magazine he called it like writing haiku (Koehler, 389). A reader in response to Jennifer Egan's short story called it a narrative poem (Ibid).

Koehler calls this phenomena the "ideological baggage." He writes:

"As Marshal McLuhan argued in Understanding Media, any cool medium is going to require the participation of its audience to fully express the potential of the medium – and as we use the vocabulary of (and ideological baggage associated with) print-based understandings of genre to understand how they blur and evolve in digital spaces – the genre category of a digital craft criticism points us toward how generic conventions are resisted (as they are in Vanishing Point) or mutated (as they are in the "live" stories of the tweeted work of Moody and Egan).

So far we saw how the process of creative writing has been transformed by digital technologies something that Koehler calls "digital craft criticism." New Age Media is blurring boundaries and affording writers of today new formats of storytelling that are at the intersection of genres and media.

2.8 Authorship in the New Age

A third aspect that digitization has changed is that of authorship. Koehler discusses originality and authorship in the digital age. He examines the idea of appropriation that content writing and creative writing in the age of Google and Internet affords the writer. A lot of the content that is written and available online today is also a rehash of existing content. The sheer volume available online is mindboggling and one can find content on almost any and every topic. Traditionally, creative writing focused on absolute creation of imaginative text. However, as mentioned above, today texts are created by assimilating a plethora of content available online. The old adage that there are no original ideas and that all creative ideas have already been thought of, seem to take on a new meaning in the online context.

Often, today's writers quote text or reproduce material or rephrase it without bothering about copyright issues. This begets the question that who is a true author and what is really creative in this creation. Nonethless, this form of creation is becoming popular and common these days.

Creative Writing 2.0

Limitations of the new age text

In the past reading was an immersive experience wherein the reader could pick up a book and become lost in it. Often going back to it again and again and finding new meanings. The reader would engage with the creative text and use their own imagination to enter the author's world. This is how works would end up becoming classics, surviving the test of time – something we talk about in chapter 4.

However, today, with all the technologies at their disposal the authors take the reader into their own mind by laying out their world through images, sounds and even videos. Is this a positive development? We are not sure. In earlier times the authors will use their command over language and their skill as story teller to describe for example a landscape. in manner that language itself will create a picture in the reads mind. This require creativity as well as skill. Now an author can creat it through image or any such medium. Far easier both for reader and author. But like any other application use of technology will make this art of storytelling may dwindle in course of time

2.9 Narratives in New Media

The meteoric growth in digital media has resulted in the ever-expanding narrative possibilities. In the book New Narratives – Stories and Storyteeling in the Digital Age, editors Ruth Page and Bronwen Thomas bring together leading theorists and practitioners of digital narratives to understand this phenomena.

As an extension, social media platforms are also bringing into existence new literary formats and changing the way storytelling is written and read. From Cell phone novels, to nanofiction to Twitterature to hypertext, literature has been reinvented. Nanofiction, a term commonly used to refer to various types of microfiction or very short writing, including that that fits the constraints of the website Twitter, also called twitterature, Twitter fiction or twiction.. The primary format of the Twitter message, or "tweet," is that it consist only of 140 characters. Twitter creators intended this format to adhere to the standards in place for SMS text messaging on phones. This format encourages you to remain brief with your content within messages, or to break up content into smaller logical pieces. Furthermore, it encourages a fast-paced exchange of posts, so that instead of long form and long-lasting messages, you instead engage through a series of short and pointed statements.

For the purposes of our research I take a look at some of these developments namely – cellphone novels and new narratives that have come about due to technology and Twitterature. In Chapter 4 I also take a look at Instagram stories to explore how these platforms are redefining creative writing. We have already taken a look so far at the change in processes, expansion of genres and a new language that has arisen to describe the new developments. Now, we take a look at some of these new narratives

1. Cellphone novels

Originally invented by a30-year-old Japanese under the pen name Yoshi, in the early 2000s, this form of storytelling has become immensely popular. Called as KetaiShousetsui, literally it means Ketai – cellphone and Shousetsu – cellphone novel. It is termed as such because its format is that of a serialized fiction novel written on a cellphone.

When Yoshi first began writing his novel there were no sites that could host his stories. So sent them as emails and messages to his readers. Subsequently, he set up a website to publish his novel – Deep Love. His novel became so popular that soon it was taken up for publishing by a publishing house selling 2. 7 million copied and was even turned into a manga (Japanese term for comics) and adapted for screen. This trend has now gained a following all over the world including India.

A break from normal author-reader relationship can be witnessed in this format since the readers are collaborators in the creation of the story. They share their feedback and even give suggestions as to what the storyline should be like to the author who even incorporates it in his story.

This collaborative feature is a constant across mediums such as Facebook posts, blog posts, Twitter and even fan literature. In the book Narratives mentioned above, researchers explore how contributions by fans and readers breaks the usual storytelling structure and creates an altogether new format.

This kind of literature, however, has its limitations, something researcher Dhananjay explores in his paper on Cellphone novels.

The fact that the stories have to fit on a cellphone screen means that they have to be readable and be of a length where the text is small (max 100-200 characters) (Dhananjay, 86).

Consequently, the sentences are very short limiting the plot and character development. It also involves usage of Emojis and other symbols specific to text messages.

This new form of language which is gaining ground even on social media, is not only helpful in saving space but is easily understandable by the readers – mostly teens in this case – and is easily accessible on phone.

Though as we discuss in the next chapter, critics and scholars of literature are raising doubts over the use of poor vocabulary, slangs and sub-standard language which is very basic. Something that is not found in the novels that win international awards, so far.

Besides this, these novels are hardly edited before being released to the public thus giving no chance to for being corrected for sentence structure, continuity or grammar. A pique that is shared across platforms. (Dhananjay, 89)

Though main line publishers and powers that be are still to take this micro-lit as a serious form of literature; the fact is this new format is here to stay and could even be the future of literature. In the meantime, it will be safe to say that this is also a form of creative writing that has evolved due to technology and adapted for it.

2. Twitterature

One of the earliest proponents of nano-fiction would be Ernest Hemmingway - An example that will be found on almost any research paper exploring this new format. Whether he would have been scandalized or would have loved to experiment on these new platforms is a question that is up for one's imagination. But the fact is he won a bet for his 6-word long story – "For sale: Baby shoes, never worn." In a way this is a precursor to the micro-lit and nano-fiction present today. Ofcourse, these have always existed in different formats but today's digitization and electronic age is providing creative writers with a wide playing field. Authors are "using short form content in fascinating new ways, marrying character count constrictions and the network effect to crowdsource stories, experiment with form and engage in direct distribution tactics." (Rudin, 2011)

Twitter started in 2006 as a medium to connect small groupsthourhg short message service of 140 characters. Once in the public domain, however, it took on a life of its own. Today, it boasts of 330 million monthly active users and 145 million daily active users and has increased its characted limit to 280. Whether one has an opinion, a status or even a story to tell, Twitter is the place to be. It is no longer confined to messages but is used to create literary gems. Its restrictions have actually given birth to a new form of creative writing, where brevity now breeds bestsellers! It boasts of a Twiiter Fiction Festival wherein known and unknown authors take a stab at greatness in 280- characters. This micro-lit – Twitterature (Rudin, 2011) has created its own micro- fandom. There are two kinds of users – those who create content and those who follow it.

Some use Twitter as a means to market their books while others have found success in landing publishing deals through their work on Twitter. Matt Stewart, one such author, tweeted his whole story, every 15 minutes on Twitter and landed a publishing deal (Rudin, 2011).

The platform can also serve as a means to attract the new reader whose attention span but allows time for microlit – towards the great classics. Penguin's Twitterature summarizes 80 of the world's leading classics in less than 20 tweets – some of its authors but 19 years old but speaking the language of their peers (Rudin, 2011).

Creating short short fiction is a work of art. Twitter fiction can be deceptively complex (Sharaqi, 2016). According to Santulli, while some Twitter stories are easy to grasp, there are others that have an entire mythos behind them (Ibid). Twitter fiction does have its critics. Some find it is an incomplete work of art by traditional standards since it does not cover the basic five elements of a story – plot, setting, character, conflict and resolution. (Ibid). At the same time, it is not the same experience as immersive reading with a book (Frankin, 2014)

Sharaqi observes: "Apparently, many writers are attracted primarily by Twitter's casual immediacy, while others are galvanized by the possibility of creating ambitious works that are fundamentally different from printed literature (Franklin, 2014). Teju Cole, the Nigerian-American writer, gained phenomenal popularity when he converted his Twitter feed into a short story template (Penny, 2014). He sifted through Nigerian newspapers for stories about especially resonant crimes to share in his single tweets (Franklin, 2014). Other renowned and best-selling authors such as Rick Moody, Jennifer Egan, and David Mitchell also started sharing their original work through micro-serialized tweets. Interestingly, two University of Chicago students, Alexander Aciman and Emmett Rensin, collaborated to share the essence of eighty of the greatest literary classics of Western literature in their book, "Twitterature." They used 2800 characters (up to 20 tweets) to tell each story."

In an interesting experiment Manoj Pandey, a writer/illustrator based out of New Delhi one day decided to tweet out a story – what followed was unprecedented. Suddenly, there were others tweeting tales right back at him including stalwarts like Salman Rushdie and SashiTharoor. In the end, he decided to publish it as a book titled Tales on Tweet, which have been illustrated as well.

This experiment brings forth another interesting aspect of Twitterature – collaboration. Readers and other authors can send suggestions and plot twists to the author who has the option to incorporate it. This form of co-authoring may not be new, but imagine if Gone with the Wind had a different ending because a reader wanted it so? Or what would be the final result if Rebecca came back to life? Does this kind of collaborating really add value? If there are leading authors maybe but then what does it say about plot construction?

Another aspect of Twitterature is the fact that one has to really wait for the next installment to appear. Though serialized fiction is nothing new. But suppose your favourite author is tweeting a story at 10 am US time and you are in India, will you stay up to read it as it come? And finally, unless all tweets are posted together or collated on a platform, searching for past tweets can be a bit of a challenge offputting for a serious reader seeking immersive experience.

Despite these minor roadblocks, people are increasingly turning to Tweet their stories or follow their favourite authors on Twitter.

3. Narratives in the Digital Age

The evolution of digital technologies has had a significant impact in the transformation of narrative theory and practice. Writings that utilize digital media for creating stories have introduced vital new territory against which narrative analysis tools can be tested and refined. (Page&Thomas, 1). By the 1990s, abundant criticism was available that made "radical claims for a narrative revolution in the light of hypertext, gaming, MUDs and MOOs" (Douglas 1992; Aarseth 1997; Landow 1997; Murray 1997; Hayles 2001). This criticism dealt with a range of narrative issues such as plot, event structures and temporality (Page&Thomas, 1) even as it debated on how such a text is experienced. However, by the beginning of the 21 century with the rapid advancement in technology a lot has changed in terms of kinds of narrative available in digital media and the tools to analyze them.

In the early stages of hyperfiction text still remained at the center, however, in what Kate Hayles (2003) describes as the second wave of digital fiction the multimodal capacity of electronic literature has been enriched. (Page&Thomas, 2) Now animation and graphics are as prominent in telling a story as is interactive interface.

Add to this the increased use of Internet, which we discuss in detail in the next chapter, has also had an impact on the narratives in new media. (ibid.) Thomas and Page make an interesting comment in that the introduction of Web 2. 0 technologies in the late 1990s have allowed even people with relatively less technical skill to manipulate, create and upload text. The rise of World Wide Web has introduced a plethora of storytelling platforms and communities as has it allowed collaboration and networking. "Other communities have emerged within the wider context of social networking sites, creating new and hybrid stories across modes and genres." (Thomas&Page, 2). For instance, Instagram is a platform which allows its users visual storytelling along with a post that has elements of text. While platforms like Medium lets its users create blogs, journals and even set up discussion boards for their works. Another platform that has since a meteoric rise is Facebook. It not only has space for collaborative storytelling but is a microblogging platform where people can post stories or create videos to go along with or a photo. It can be said safely that the there are as many storytelling and new narratives as there are platforms. Narrative forms continue to expand with technology and become obsolete just as fast. Just like the hypertext fiction of the first wave of digital narratology.

New Media

In this context, I would like to talk about New Media narrative, in his essay From Synesthesia to Multimedia – How to talk about New Media Narrative, Daniel Punday talks about the challenge of interpreting new media texts and observes that what it requires is developing native categories and terms that are fair to this medium, (Thomas&Page, 19) something that we discussed above in the context of using existing categories to describe the new texts created. Though he does comment that new media and traditional narrative are not really independent (Ibid). New media is characterized by variability and interactivity observes Marie-Laure Ryan (Thomas&Page, 35). One of the most interesting element of digital text is its interactivity. Instead of a pre- determined narrative by an author content in the digital space such as blogs, Facebook posts offer the reader to become a co-creator of text.

"Aristotle (1996) wrote the rules for traditional drama in his Poetics but there is to this day no poetics and no set of guidelines for interactive drama." (Ibid, 49)

Fan fiction

The most famous example of this would be the hundreds of fan fiction site that emerged post Harry Potter or the most famous Vampire. Though the beginning of a fan fiction site presupposed the existence of a text, it takes of from there in different directions. Bronwen Thomas in his essay "Update Soon!" Harry Potter Fanfiction and narrative as a participatory process defines fanfiction as "prose fiction of any length, style, genre, and narrative technique produced by fans of aeide wide range of cultural products including TV shoes, movies, video games, Japanese manga, and 'classic' literature. (Thomas, Thomas&Page, 205). Thomas explores the extent of collaboration that such sites offer. He observes that Page's and Pugh's research on such blog reveal that not many of the authors incorporate the suggestions made to them by the readers of the site which they leave in the comments on the stories uploaded by them. However, Thomas differs from this view. He notes that often the authors who update text on such sites acknowledge the influence and contribution of others thus suggesting some degree of influence. (Thomas, Thomas&Page, 213). Thomas parks fanfiction into the catgory of a new narrative due to its inherent process of review and updating. He also observes that every thing that the author writes is up for debate and the reader is an equal contributor to stories via their comments. Fanfiction contests the idea of both text as under the ownership of one individual as it does of the text as something stable and finished (Thomas, Thomas&Page,

217). Authors are perceived not as god-like slogging away in isolation and inspired but as participants. And text including the source text up for modification. Finally, reading pleasure is not limited to one text but dispersed across "texts, categories and genres." (Thomas, Thomas&Page, 217).

These aspects clearly point towards a new form of creative writing and process distinct from that understood in the traditional sense.

In closing, the words of Janet H. Murray who wrote the path breaking work Hamlet on the Holodeck – The Future of Narrative in Cyberspace, seem apt "computation offers a powerful new set of expressive affordances for the ancient human activity of storytelling." (Murray, Preface)

CHAPTER III

SOCIAL MEDIA AND LITERATURE

Overview

In the last chapter we explored what creative writing has come to mean in the context of the technological evolution that we are witnessing in the current times. We saw how narratives are transforming given the technological advancement.

In this chapter we trace the evolution of technologies like internet and social media platforms and impact these technologies have on English Language.

We have already taken a detailed look at how these platforms are changing the literary form.

A rising concern with these platforms has been the distortion of the English language. The aim of social media is to stay in touch and communicate, with speed being of the essence. This has led to new developments in the English language which exasperate the purists but is the norm for communication for the Generation Z and now Alpha – those that are called digital natives.

In this case the question that arises is that do we need to balance the need to express and temper it with some sort of correction in order to maintain the sanctity of the language; Or do we need to absorb and accept the new lingo as the next step in evolution of English.

According to Prof. Ing. Klaus (2017) the author of the book The Fourth Industrial Revolution, all new developments and technologies have one key feature in common – they leverage the persuasive power of digitization and information technology. So, whether we like it or not this development will stay. And, in fact, in the future we will see more interventions of Artificial Intelligence (AI).

The technology is progressing so fast that Kristian Hammond (2019), co- founder of Narrative Science, a company specializing in automated narrative generation, forecasts that by the mid-2020s, 90% of news could be generated by an algorithm, most of it without any human intervention. So, we attempt to take a look at some of the concerns and changes in language and creative writing apropos these developments have raised and what we can do about it.

With the advent of computers and the digital technological evolution we moved into third industrial revolution somewhere past the middle of 19th century The humanity is now in the midst of the Fourth Industrial revolution. It has impacted every area of human life, blurring the lines between "the physical, digital and biological worlds in ways that create both huge promise and potential peril."(World Economic Forum, 2020)

One of the areas going through the pangs of tremendous evolution is human language. Research is being conducted on how technological advances are transforming languages. However, in this study an endeavor is made to see as to what has been the impact of technology on creative writing in English and on the language itself.

The idea is to look at existing research as is available in the public domain, and understand how far we have been able to truly comprehend the change being brought about and to assess if a model can be reified to replace what has been called the "gatekeepers of quality" in the past.

Over the years, evolution in creative writing has enriched the literature with a new voice, representing the coming of age of a generation that saw the advent of Internet and the myriad platforms that came into existence due to the same. In today's times, digital tools affect writing in significant ways including broadening the audience for the amateur authors and encouraging collaboration amongst them virtually. Online platforms allow writers to work alongside and edit each other's work resulting in instant peer review.

On the flip side, however, there is an increasing danger of informality creeping into creating writing standards as a result of colloquial and informal usage of the diction. Add to this the incapacity of today's "quick authors" to navigate complicated texts, and handle copyright and related issues in their compositions.

3.1 The digital technologies and their evolution in context to creative writing

The internal mechanics of technologies like internet, social media platforms, smartphones, artificial intelligence, network coverage 3G, 4G and 5G etc which have impacted our daily life, is complex and beyond the comprehension of normal user. These technologies have inter-alia impacted the creative writing in a manner which is considered paradigm shift in the manner creative writing was traditionally was viewed as. This of course is the subject matter of this thesis However, as we discuss the impact of these technologies on creative writing we cannot help avoiding the reference to these technologies. Some of them like internet, social media platforms, artificial intelligence are directly referred to, whereas others may be required to be referred while explaining these technologies. Dealing with issues arising out of the impact of this technology on creative writing, an "awareness" or "appreciation" of this technology is necessary. We have deliberately used the word "awareness" or "appreciation" in respect to these technologies, which should be adequate for our purpose. Therefore, what follows is an explanation on these technologies in a language which makes sense to ordinary reader. The explanation which follow primarily focuses on "What these technologies are", "how they evolved", "present status of development" and "What future look like"

The Rise of the Internet

Basically the Internet is a network of computers that are able to communicate to each other using a protocol that is popularly known as the TCP/IP suite. TCP/IP stands for Transmission Control Protocol/Internet Protocol. TCP/IP is a set of standardized rules that allow computers to communicate on a network such as the internet.

Cyber space is another terminology which needs some explanation before we continue further with Internet. While internet is a network of networks, that it is a global network that is being created by linking smaller networks of computers and servers, Cyber-space on the other hand is nothing more than a symbolic and figurative space that exists within the scope of Internet. It can be said that anything that is done via the use of Internet, occurs within the confines of the cyber-space, whether that is sending an e-mail, a website, or playing a game, all of these things exist within the cyber-space. The term cyberspace has led to the introduction of other words, such as cyber security, cyber-crime, cyber-war, cyber-terrorism, etc.

The Internet, a complex and revolutionary invention, came into being in 1965. Though its origins can be traced back to work done in the 1940s (Springer), started by computer specialists in Europe. This was soon utilized by the Defense personnel in the USA to create a national communications system. From there it slowly got introduced in campuses. However, it was in 1989, the English scientist Tim Berners Lee brought in the revolutionary concept and began to create a system that he would come to call the "World Wide Web" (commonly known as the Web). Before the invention of the World Wide Web, accomplishing anything on internet was a real chore. The information on the internet was difficult to search for, and almost impossibly dense. The pre-Web Internet was an almost entirely text-based world. The development by Tim Berner l started rather innocently. In 1989, some scientists at CERN, the science research center in Switzerland, wanted to automatically share their information with fellow scientists working elsewhere in the world. Email already existed, but there was no easy way to transmit large amounts of data other than saving it on a disk and physically bringing it to another computer.

So Berners-Lee, a researcher working at CERN, created the World Wide Web. It solved the communication problem for the scientists—and changed human existence as we know it.

The internet and the World Wide Webis not the same thing. The internet is a huge network of computers all connected together. The World Wide Web ('www' or 'web' for short) is a collection of webpages found on this network of computers. The web browser uses the internet to access the web.

Tim suggested three main technologies that meant all computers could understand each other (HTML, URL and HTTP). All of these remain in use today.

However, it was in 1991 that this actually became publically accessible. And since then there has been no looking back.

The World Wide Web opened up the internet to everyone.

It connected the world in a way that was not possible before and made it much easier for people to get information, share and communicate.

It allowed people to share their work and thoughts through social networking sites, blogs and video sharing.

The World Wide Web made it much easier for people to share information.

Web 2. 0

As the web began to develop, people started communicating and sharing more. They used social network sites and blogs. It became much easier to create your own content on the web and to share it. This new type of web became known as Web 2. 0. (Traditional Web retroactively referred to as Web 1. 0)

There are number of different types of web 2. 0 applications including wikis, blogs, social networking, folksonomies, podcasting & content hosting services.

The term was invented by Darcy DiNucci in 1999 and later popularized by Tim O'Reilly and Dale Dougherty at the O'Reilly Media Web 2. 0 Conference in late 2004.

Familiar examples of Web 2. 0 sites and tools include wikis and blogs (PBworks and WordPress), social networking sites (Facebook and Twitter), image and video hosting sites (Flicker and YouTube), and applications to generate Web content for education, business, and social purposes (Wikipedia, Weebly, and Instagram).

Move to a smartphone dominated the world

While the advent of broadband and the internet as we know it today has revolutionized the way that people connect to the internet, Mobile broadband— connecting to the internet through a cell phone—has exploded in popularity over the last decade.

The mobile network technologies

Cellular data is a term that means connecting to the Internet using a cellular phone network. That means one can access the Internet while moving away from Wi- Fi.

Cellular data is very important as a mobile phone. A mobile phone can do wonders, but without mobile data, your smartphone is just like any other regular phones.

The mobile networks that we know today have evolved continuously since their inception nearly 40 years ago. 1G, 2G, 3G, 4G and 5G represent the five generations of mobile networks where G stands for 'Generation' and the numbers 1, 2, 3, 4 and 5 represent the generation number. Since the early 1980s, almost every ten years, we have seen a new generation of mobile networks.

With 3G, smartphones generally see download speeds of up to around 2Mbps (megabits per second). By comparison, 4G is around 3 to 5Mbps; roughly the speed that many home computers receive via cable modem or DSL. 5G's peak download speed is up to 20, 480 Mbps, a huge leap from any generation previously. With a higher network generation comes higher capacity, meaning it can support a greater number of users at any given time. It will also allow for higher data rates, so that multimedia applications such as video calling or YouTube clips work more smoothly.

The difference between these generations is simply a network that improves upon the previous internet experience – not that 4G is twice as good as 3G.

4G is more spectrally efficient than 3G, just as 5G is more spectrally efficient than 4G. Each generation delivers more data per hertz than the previous one. 3G works at frequencies up to 2. 1Gigahertz, 4G up to 2. 5Gigahertz and 5G can be up to 95 Gigahertz. That is why there is a lot of hype around 5G. The 5th generation wireless network addresses the evolution beyond mobile internet to massive IoT (Internet of Things). The capabilities of the network are so much faster than in previous generations and can therefore connect more objects than ever before, including things like connected vehicles, connected homes and smart cities,

To Sum UP

The speed with which information is stored, shared, retrieved irrespective of one's location has transformed the world completely, leading to applications in diverse areas.

Advent of the Social Media Platforms

Internet also began to transform the way we communicated with each other replacing the 'handwritten letters' of the past. Let us briefly trace the origin of the Social Media platforms. First the Internet Relay Chats in 1988, which was the precursor of today's social media. The first recognizable Social Media site is said to be Six Degrees created in 1997. While it was in 1999 that the blogging sites started to appear and become popular. Soon after this, the social media really took off rapidly and replaced the way in which we all used to be connected with each other. Letters had already been replaced by the e-mails, which were getting replaced by instant messages and posts. People increasingly started using these to keep in touch and to exchange information on a daily basis and instantly.

Definition of Social Media

Merriam Webster Dictionary (2020) defines social media as "forms of electronic communication (such as websites for social networking and micro blogging) through which users create online communities to share information, ideas, personal messages and other content (such as videos).

Social media can be defined as forms of electronic communication through which users interact among people in which they create, freely share, exchange and discuss information, ideas, personal messages, and other content about each other and their lives using a multimedia mix of personal words, pictures, videos and audio, utilizing online platforms while they are connected to the Internet (Cox &Rethman, (2011). Since their appearance, social media have changed different aspects of people's lives. Social media that were emerged by the rise of Web 2. 0 technologies are characterized by several significant features such as user generated content, online identity creation and relational networking (Margo, 2012).

3.2 Impact on English Language

As mentioned above today, we are connected to these platforms not just via desktops and laptops but smartphones as well. An interesting byproduct of this phenomenon, crucial for our purposes, is the change that started to be seen in the language people used to communicate with one another. Since the speed of response became crucial, people started to use --

- Misspellings,
- Alien jargons,
- Emojis,
- New abbreviations, and
- In some cases irrespective of the grammar being used –

This led to the birth of what came to be known as Internet slang. Eventually, these slangs percolated down into verbal communication as accepted forms of language.

The New English

Social media is here to stay. Each of its platforms has millions of subscribers and followers and they are only increasing. They are replacing news sites and are being used for advertising and sharing knowledge and opinions in creative ways. They are the 'new creative writing' and 'communication' tools. As we mentioned earlier, each of these have given birth to certain language trends which can be broadly categorized as:

Redefining creative writing

Creative writing has three major components –

- The craft,
- The process
- And what we like to call as 'the gatekeeping. '

Creative writing is anything that goes beyond professional, journalistic, academic or technical forms of literature. (Wiki, 2020) It is an expression of human creativity and is also an expression of an individual's experience as well. For our purpose, we can take a look at how Graeme Harper defines Creative Writing in the digital context. He mentions in his book, The Future of Creative Writing (2014), "Creative writing involves both the use of language and contributions to language. As a medium largely dependent upon written language, and with a complex and ever- changing relationship with spoken language too, even at the level of words being placed on a page (whatever kind of "page" that might be: paper, electronic, other), creative writing is heavily impacted upon by language change."

The craft is essentially a matter of the creator's imagination and language skills. The process here refers to factors that influence the creator. An author (and I use this term for the sake of the paper for poets and other writers of this genre) is as much a product of his/her socio-political environment as he/she influences it. Add to this equation- technology now. Does a digital platform impact an author's way of creating his piece? When publishing moves from traditional paper to digital platform does it change the written piece? For instance, with technology, a piece of written work today can be a combination of pictures, music, links to other works or even hyperlinking within the text, completely changing the genre itself (Koehler 2013). In an interesting experiment, Rick Moody, a famous scriptwriter wrote the first Twitter short story in 154 characters in 2009. The experiment raised several questions - how does one trace the plot, character and timeline in small snippets that could involve active participation by readers too? Would it firmly come within the scope of creative writing? Or for that matter consider the use of hashtags on Instagram that are equally important to build a narrative on the platform.

The third essential arm of creative writing is that of the gatekeepers – a term and concept that we are transposing from scholarly writing to our framework. These are the editors and publishers who are the doyens of language and ensure a written piece is in line with what we understand correct language to be. The problem with social media platforms is that these do not have any authentic way to check 'improper English usage' or its grammar resulting in introduction of errors and informality in written English, which eventually creeps into verbal language. As English language evolves, it not only impacts creative writing, but writers also influence the evolution of language. Which is exactly what we are observing today?

The invention of Internet slangs – This consist of new terms that have come about due to social media platforms and now find their way in dictionaries too (Horobin 2018). Add to this abbreviations and acronyms that have come to invade the way we Speak and even Write in English today. Take for instance the much popular ROFL or a LOL. Or new words like memes, unfriend, etc. It has also given rise to new dictionaries such as Urban Dictionary, which has become the one-stop shop for all internet slang.

Coining of new words is a distinctive feature of digital platforms and electronic discourse including clipped forms, blends and misspellings or respellings (Horobin, 102). However, as Horobin points out in the past objections were raised when the word television a blend of Greek telos and Latin visio was done (Ibid, 103). But it is widely accepted even today.

Rise of Emojis - What can be said in one sentence can now be expressed in an emoji (Novak et al. 1, 2015). In fact, Professor John Sutherland (2015) from University College London predicts that rise of emojis could be the next evolution in language. He mentions that this tendency of humans to communicate can be traced back to the caveman's mode of communication in drawings. In fact, emoticon is a way to add tone to a message or a post. Emojis were first used by Japanese teens in the 1990s in their pagers, however, today entire messages can be conveyed by these "smileys". (Horobin, 109). Horobin in his book on the English language cites the example of a crowd-sourced project that transformed the entire Moby Dick into emojis, though with limitations. (Ibid)

Appropriation (or as some researchers call it re-appropriation) of vocabulary – This refers to the trend wherein a particular word, though it means something specific, has come to take on a new meaning given the context of application (Dalzell & Victor, 2017). For instance, page which indicated a particular place in a published book can now mean a webpage. Or Wall, which traditionally meant a brick wall, could now indicate a Facebook page. Or for that matter platforms, have now come to mean social media sites.

Breakdown of silos – Though the world could still be divided between British English and American English, now online, these distinctions are blurring.

Generation Language Gap – This refers to a new phenomenon wherein the language that a millennial or Gen. Y uses to communicate in, may be alien to someone in his or her middle age - Think parent and child. This is an insight that a study led by Professor Sutherland (2015) also found.

The English Language – Tracing its journey till today

In his very interesting and short book, The English Language – A Very Brief Introduction, Simon Horobin traces the evolution of the English language over the centuries.

English began its journey as a member of the Germanic language family as can be traced to the earliest records. Since the Old English Period, though, it witnessed numerous changes that substantially changed its structure, vocabulary, pronunciation and even spelling.

Over the years, it continued to be influenced by other languages, borrowing words from them such as from French. This was the result of a number of factors including but not limited to trade and travel, major social upheavels, and its changing role in society. (Horobin, 31) Although, the fact that the language borrows words from foreign sources rather than Old English is a much debated topic even today especially by proponents of pure English.

Horobin notes that the attempts to create a purer form of English can be traced back to the 16th century. (Horobin, 7) However, with the language being one of the leading ones used for communication across the world, it is impossible for it not to recognize and incorporate foreign words. This can be seen with the introduction of Indian words like chutney in the Oxford dictionary. With globalization and now the internet spread, to isolate the language will not be easy.

Be that is may, what about adding abbreviations into the mix? Like we read about Urban Dictionary earlier, with the rising popularity of social media of English, should these also find a place in the English of today. Horobin cites and interesting example to explore this point. He talks of how in 2005 the Bible Society of Australia commissioned a project to make the Bible more accessible to the youngsters by translating it into a version that used "abbreviations typical of SMS texting." (Horobin, 9) He raises some pertinent question related to this type of English. Does this herald the emergence of a new kind of English, or are such creative reworkings merely a passing fad? Is this an acceptable form of communication, or a corruption of correct English spelling and grammar? By giving text speech legitimacy in this way, are we accepting lower standards of literacy, and thereby condemning future generations to a lifetime of underachievement? Or is this how we will all be writing English in the future, as digital media become increasingly central to learning and communication?" (Horobin, 9)

Today, slang words or those gaining acceptance due to widespread usage are being included in dictionaries. Though this may be a point of consternation for some, the fact that they are part of regular parlance should make these inclusions relevant.

We saw some of the changes in language that have been brought about by platforms. There has been much debate on the fact that this medium gives itself to linguistic poverty and that it is corrupting the language as a whole. However, quite a few of the trends that we saw above can be traced to pre-electronic era too.

For instance, the usage of the prefix "un" as a negative marker was widespread in Old English. Even today a similar thought process lies behind words like unfollow or unfriend – terms coined by Twitter and Facebook. Blending two words to create 'portmanteau words' is not new either (Horobin, 104). Moving on to acronyms and initialisms – even they can trace back their origins in history. Take for example OMG (oh My God) which can be traced back by OED to 1917! (Horobin, 104). The introduction of smartphones with full keyboards has made logograms like CU and L8R less common in texting (Ibid). Another common feature of communication on social media is "verbing," "by which a word shifts its class without any change in form." Example – Google it meaning look it up. (Ibid). However, even this trend is not new, with rain, action, dialogue being conversions of this kind.

Horobin sheds light on a lesser observed trend as a result of communication on social media – use of punctuation. It has in fact resulted in an entirely new convention for punctuation. As we've observed elsewhere in this research communicating on social media or electronically is real-time, with no chance for revision, or editing. Talking about this Horobin says:

"It is this blending of features of speech and writing that has prompted David Crystal to characterize texting as 'speaking with your fingers. ' What appears to be a random and ignorant misapplication of the standard repertoire of punctuation marks in electronic discourse is, on closer examination, more often a s sophisticated attempt to convey the attitudinal and emotional information typically associated with speech in written medium." (Horobin, 108)

The only drawback of this form of communication is that there is no way of knowing when something is being written in anger or in a regular manner. Though an accepted practice is that using all caps in messages or communication is considered a form of shouting.

Framework required for correct usage

Language is considered as a living thing. It changes and evolves as humans do. When Shakespeare wrote his works he wrote in the language of the common man of that time but today only classic theater practitioners use his language for a play. Similarly, a writer is pretty much free to write in the language of his times. In fact, during the Renaissance period of Europe, the English poets and playwrights like Shakespeare are credited with inventing thousands of new words and idioms, which continue to be part of our language even today. Not only that we see the lexicographers of Oxford Dictionary incorporating many Indian words which have become common today worldwide. However, they indicate the origin in parenthesis.

If we trace the evolution of English language we see how it has been transformed into its new avatar - from Anglo-Saxon to the abbreviated versions of the preset times and continues to evolve further.

So, why would this evolution be any different? The only problem is that we are still to start communication in 'improper English' officially. New forms of language may have entered everyday jargon but we still do not like to read a book or even an email or a Facebook post that has incorrect use of English language. The important thing today is to be able to create a framework where the authored pieces going out on social media can be corrected for structure and grammar before being posted online.

Though Twitter and Instagram have features where you can report inappropriate posts but that do not include incorrect grammar. Not only that with Apps like Grammarly becoming popular many times auto-correct becomes an option but it is not always accurate.

So, what we need is still a way to express our creativity in the terms of proper rules of grammar of English. This is something we explore more in Chapter 5.

Conclusion

The Dgital Revolution is transforming the way we communicate with each other including the language we use to do so. The Internet and social media platforms are the new communication tools and are here to stay. However, there is still a need to ensure that the English language used while incorporating the new elements has also to read correctly. For this a framework that can replicate the function of editors on social media platforms is required. What we need are moderators that would only allow publication if certain rules of language are met or, if the need arises, to collapse the uploaded material completely. Though language is alive and evolves with time, we are at a crossroads where either we are able to retain the 'sanctity of English language' or agree to the transformation it is undergoing even if it implies breakdown of age-old linguistic parameters as we know it. After all, at the end of the day, language is a means to communicate and be understood. And if the new trends are being accepted and embraced by the millennials and Gen Y, then would 'correct English' and creative writing really come to mean something new.

Horobin sums it best: "Far from being an impoverished medium, electronic communication is characterized by creativity and playfulness, spawning new words, and repurposing traditional conventions of spelling and punctuation. Since emails, tweets and text messages are intended to be short missives written in haste, without requiring the proofreading and revision that are commonly applied to more formal writing, it is not surprising that they commonly include spelling, punctuation and typographical errors... To view such features as evidence of illiteracy is to make the same mistake as judging dialect speech according to the conventions of standard written English. While it remains inappropriate to adopt a similarly relaxed attitude towards spelling, punctuation and grammar in formal written English, this is an accepted aspect of electronic discourse. Attempts to police electronic usage and to insist its users follow conventional rules seems doomed to failure." (109-110)

CHAPTER IV

THE TIMES OF OVER INFORMATION AND ITS DARK SIDE

Overview

Classics in literature are outstanding works of creative writing, the works which have touched and provoked the sentiments of readers. The classics are not limited to literary fiction, which some people often do. Each genre and category of literature or creative writing has its own classics. The classic literature was outstanding work itself, when it was created. However, over a period of time it was read and reread by millions of readers. In some cases, it was translated into many different languages. In other words, its popularity among the readers over a stretch of time established its credentials as classic.

The other approach in defining a work in English as classic or outstanding work in creative writing could be to provide a list of criteria which must be met. This chapter explores the views of different critics and authors in an effort to establish such criteria. This chapter will also explore whether certain category of creative narratives on digital media can at all meet some of these criteria.

1.1 TRADITIONAL DEFINITION OF A CLASSIC - Criteria

What is a classic? T. S. Eliot and J. M. Coetze explored this question in their lectures 47 years apart in the 20th century. Before we delve into their exploration of this timeless question, it would be interesting to see what constitutes a classic work. If we look closely, we will find that classic is one part skill and one part the emotions it evokes in a reader; though the latter is a matter of subjective judgment.

In her paper "What is a classic?: International Literary Criticism and the Classic Question," Mukherjee (2010) observes that "classic" pertain to the literature that survives critical questioning. It is like the canonical work, a book that is read long even after it has been written for quite some time and still qualifies for a good read in the present time. Though Mukherjee (2010) explores the classics in context with literary criticism, the essay highlights of an essential criteria of a classic, its timelessness.

There are many other factors that transform any written work into a classic. In his work discussing the ancient Chinese Book of Changes, Richard J. Smith puts forward a definition of a classic which is also corroborated in the work of Italian writer Calvino (2014) in his book "Why Read the Classics?" If we read these points closely, we sense that a classic is as much about the skill of the author as it is about a reader's experience. For instance, he says, "A classic is a book which with each rereading offers as much of a sense of discovery as the first reading". He further says, "The classics are those books which come to us bearing the aura of previous interpretations, and trailing behind them the traces they have left in the culture or cultures (or just in the languages and customs) through which they have passed." This brings us to the next aspect of a classic, that they are the product of the socio-political and historical epoch in which they exist. As we know, an author is a by-product of his times and is as much influenced by it as he influences it. It is because the writer assimilates and comments on what he sees and thus puts down eternal truths, that they connect with the reader and leave such an imprint on their imagination that it refuses to leave them. Even Eliot (1945) says that, "it is only by hindsight and in the historical perspective that a classic can be known as such". This implies that often a classic is termed so by history and when it stands the test of time. Sometimes in their own era of existence they may not achieve the cult status that time ascribes to them.

Mukherjee (2010) states that, "a classic occurs when a civilization and a language and literature are mature and there is a community of taste and a common style". This is supported by Elliot who also stated that "A mature literature has a historical trajectory behind it, the history of 'an ordered though unconscious progress of a language to realize its own potentialities within its own limitations'".

What these explain is that a classic not only takes in the sweep of the past, present and future but is steeped in the living language of its times. As we observed above, an author is a by-product of the times he lives in and by that same stretch also expresses himself in the language of his times. After all, if we start writing in Shakespearean English, other than for research purposes, no one will understand us. More importantly, that is not the "living language" of the current time.

Saint Beuve (1850) opines "What is a classic? And while exploring this question records that the word was first used in ancient Rome as "classici" to describe the citizens of the first class. Thus, the word as a mode of classification originally equated social and literary rank. In his 1858 lecture he offered several definitions of the classic. He describes it as among other things as something that constantly renews itself; is a living entity; is new and ancient in equal measures."

This throws an interesting mix into the equation of a classic. It characterizes it as a living entity that stays ever relevant. That means that it is as much a contemporary of the modern literature as it was in its own time with each new generation ascribing a new interpretation and meaning to it.

- If try to summarise some of the criteria discussed above, they can be briefly as belowone-part skill and one part the emotions
- Its timelessness
- Skill of the author as it is about a reader's experience
- The product of the socio-political and historical epoch in which they
  exist.
- They connect with the reader and leave such an imprint on their imagination that it refuses to leave them.

One point clearly emerges that if we want to evaluate piece of creative writing when it is created as to whether it is outstanding piece of literature it is no easy task. The aspect of assessment of creativity seems to be a problematic to the extent that whether creative writing can be assessed is a big question mark.

1.2 ADVENT OF THE INTERNET AND E-PUBLISHING – Changing idea of a classic

The Internet, a complex and revolutionary invention, came into being in 1965. Today, it has become the mainstay of modern life. The term e-publishing was introduced by William Dijkhuis in 1977 and the first e-publication was plain text emails (Velmurugan&Natarajan, 2015). Through the e-platform, "books, short stories, collections and works of non-fiction" can be published (Velmurugan&Natarajan, 2015).

The new technologies that have developed have impacted the art of creating or composing itself. Koehler (2013), in his paper "Digitizing Craft: Creative Writing Studies and New Media: A Proposal," discussed the impact of the digital technologies on composing. With e-publishing, hypertext and now new media, multimedia and non-linear narratives have come into fashion. Koehler while tracing the emergence of 2. 0

technologies, observes how creative writers rode the wave of technological advancement and how "digital technologies redefine the boundaries we draw around fiction, poetry and non-fiction" (Koehler, 2013). Technologies are redefining genres as well.

Add to this social media platforms and blogging sites, and you have new form of authorship altogether. Let us take an example. If we look at Instagram, one of the handles on it ran a campaign called "Terribly Tiny Tales." This was a work of fiction by readers, where they submitted their new format of stories, rightly called tiny, in the form of text messages or poetry or prose, and editors selected the best ones to feature on the handle. They were expressed in the new "English language" of today and ran for a short period of time becoming immensely popular across platforms including Facebook, so people could read it where they wanted. In such a case, how do we distinguish which piece of work is a classic?

Let's take the example of another social media platform, Twitter, a microblogging platform which allows only 280 characters for people to write in. It was initially created for people to post their statuses but has now become a popular tool for narratives. In their essay "Character Development," Franklin &Maayan (2014), explore these interesting phenomena. They write about the first fiction festival held by the site. Popular and well-known authors participated in it. They 'tweeted' their stories which readers could read and 'retweet'. Though it did not get the best traction when it was introduced, today, writers around the world produce original work on it (Franklin &Maayan, 2014). However, the essayists raise the question as to whether the works being produced on the platform can come under the purview of literature as we know it.

Now, imagine for a moment that your favorite author is to tweet his or her book, as amply explained in the essay, some of us will have to stay up way past midnight just to be in the same time zone to catch every installment. Also, since tweets are posted one at a time, it breaks one's reading experience since unless re-tweeted in one go, or collected on an external platform, you cannot really find all the tweets together. Further, readers can comment and retweet on the author's work. But the question is will the retweets exert the same impact as the original composition. An important aspect of reading is getting immersed in the book, with a tweet how would it possible? Or for that matter, with hundreds or thousands of tweets being posted everyday, and some becoming trending for the day, week or month, how will you find your "classic"? How does a disappearing piece of work become timeless or be re-read or reinterpreted in every new era, as a classic is meant to be? As Franklin &Maayan (2014) observe with ample examples, that it could be that Twitter is more a way of experimenting with a platform and it mostly lends itself to be a marketing tool for an author's actual book.

Social media platforms are also transforming the English Language as we know it. We are in midst of what may be the most exciting times of evolution in a language. Due to the Internet and platforms, new forms of language are emerging as fast as they are going out of fashion. The need to communicate with speed has resulted in the breakdown of grammar rules and the emergence of a new form, which is an amalgamation of Emojis, Internet slang and abbreviations. In fact there are authors writing today who use the new language in their works. The question is will these trends stand the test of time? Is it possible to identify a classic whose language may be incomprehensible after a few decades? Though the very identity of a classic says yes, only time will tell if that happens so.

1.3 Classics over the years

So far we have discussed the criteria that could be applied to a text to understand if it makes a classic. In an attempt to see the evolution of literature over the years, we take a look at some of the well-known authors and works of the past and at some of the popular authors writing on the new age medium – specifically social media – today, to see what are the consistencies that can be found in content, irrespective of the medium – to declare a work as a classic.

Rebecca Daphne Du Maurier Maurier calls her novel a study in jealous. The novel cleverly deals with insecurity, love and jealousy all timeless emotions. In fact by not naming the narrator the author draws the reader into the world of the characters. A Gothic masterpiece wrongly called a Romance novel when it was released. Its timelessness attests to the cutting-edge writing of Maurier and the chords she touches in her reader's hearts through her novel.

Gone With the Wind Margaret Mitchell Hailed as a literary masterpiece, the novel won the Pulitzer prize in its time. Its depiction of American society during the Civil War is very accurate considering the author did not live during the period. The story talks of survival, conflict and love through the main character Scarlett. Its depiction of the relationshio between the Rhett Butler and Scarlett, especially after their marriage is like a case study in what a couple can go through during crisis and how not communicating enough and egos can destroy good relationships. It also shows how not letting go in time can lead to missed chances and opportunities. A favourite even after decades, it shows the power of timeless truths and their connection with readers.

Kafka on the Shore Haruko Murakami A much-loved author who is popular across the world – Murakami's books take the ordinary and thrust them in the world of extraordinary, touching people's lives everywhere. In Kafka on the Shore, one of his many popular novels themes such as growth, recovery from trauma and the redemption value of suffering and explored through the concept of time viewed philosophically (Virginia Yeung). These themes are what makes his work popular with readers despite him writing in Japanese.

Laila Premchand A pioneer of short story writing he was a powerful critic of the Indian society in the late 19th and 20th century. His stories brought to light not only the plight of the downtrodden but of women during that time. In Laila he tells the story of a woman who is an ideal ruler due to her pro-poor sympathies but he does not give her an independent status instead ties her to her husband, pretty much reflecting the place of women in a patriarchal society, fighting against limitations in their given circumstances. Given that he is still popular in India today, is because his message resonates in a society still at war with itself on many fronts including gender.

An Equal Music Vikram Seth Another prolific writer of poems, travelougues and moving novels, Vikram Seth in An Equal Music takes us on a journey through the lives of two musicians in love with each other. Again, we see strains of love, loss and reconciliation while also exploring the world of professional music and its associated problems and themes. A love story in an unusual setting it is as much an allegory as a commentary, drawing us in with its power of storytelling.

Crime and Punishment Fyodor Dostovesky A controversial masterpiece, its place in world literature cannot be questioned. It takes the reader into the mind of a criminal making us see his perspective and in a way complicit in his crime. Nonetheless, this psychological masterpiece which lays out the mental anguish and morals dilemmas of the central character. It throws as many questions on society, morals and religion as it answers – forcing the reader into a debate rather than being a straightforward murder story. Again, ideas reflected in the novel and its eerie observation on society holds true even today as when it did when it was written.

Jane Eyre Charlotte Bronte Anyone who has ever experienced childhood loss and trauma cannot but be affected by this novel. A personal favorite, the travails of the central character as she is forced into the lives of relatives after her parent's death and their abuse of her is moving. From there we see her journey into an orphanage and find unusal courage in strange circumstances for a child and form friendships that become family. However, even there she faces loss and finally we see her flowering into this woman about to make a place for herself in the world. The book takes a look at issues of class discrimination, status of women who were not allowed to stand up to society in historical England and the antiquated notions of that time. Though her meeting Mr Rochester seems like an end to all problems, he also betrays her by hiding the truth about his wife which she finds out at the time of her marriage. In a society when all this would have crushed a woman we see Jane rise again and finally find herself, without leaning on a man. It is as much a story of resilience and personal struggle of a woman against society and her circumstances as it is about love. In the end we see Jane in a position of power as she takes care of an injured Rochester, on her terms, not a weak woman but one of strength. Again, a story that has stood the test of time with its message of women empowerment and of highlighting the position of women in a society much against them.

Catcher in the Rye JD Salinger A book that was written for the adults actually gained popularity with the teens because of its addressing themes like angst, alienation and superficiality of society. It was even banned at one time cause of use of excessive vulgar language and sexual content. A classic nonetheless it is popular even today.

* Please note the books chosen below are the researcher's personal favorites and based on online search.

Though choice of classics in above discussion is limited, but one common thread which stands out conspicuously is the subject matter of the story which stands relevant even today.

1.4 New Age Authors

From discussion of some of the classics over the decades and what has led to their popularity we now move on the new age platforms and authors writing on them. In our discussion we have tried to explore what makes a work a classic. Not in the sense of literary criticism but from the point of readers and their choices.

It is a well-known fact that reading is a very solitary and personal, immersive experience. People fall into a book and are drawn in. One of the elements of reading is continuity and narrative so that attention is not broken. That is why people often "stay up all night" to finish a book they love. Another aspect of a popular, well-loved book is when we can go back to it again and again and discover new meanings or insights or alternatively, re-discover what we fell in love with in the first place. A lot of the classics we talked in the table above firmly fall into this criteria. Whether it be the language or editing everything draws a reader in and introduces them to a seamless experience. When it comes to language they can often be written in the language spoken in those times and does not necessarily have to be so correct that it meets purists definition of it. Case in point "The Catcher in the Rye."

Moving on from traditional published books, we saw in chapter 1 2 how narratives have changed due to technology and as Katherine Hayes in her Writing Machines says, both the reading experience and writing have transformed due to digitization. Authors now have new technologies and platforms to play with and write on and often they find their authors there. Of course, these platforms have their own challenges, but despite that they are gaining followers of their works. One of the downsides of being a social media platform author is being known worldwide. Unless you have used the right hashtags or are known for your traditionally published works how will you find new audiences. Whereas for the traditional classics time and word of mouth as well as being acknowledged by readers over the years as a favorite made it into a classic. Going back to my own argument, since we are still living in the midst of the epoch where these platforms are on the rise and its been just a decade or so from the time they came into existence, time is still on their side. Maybe they will end up as classics in the long-run. This is because the technological evolution is not going away.

In fact, we are yet to live through and find out how technology is going to transform our lives. Philosophers like Yuval Noah Harari are studying these phenomena. In his book Homo Deus, Harari writes, "This relentless flow of data sparks new inventions and disruptions that nobody plans, controls or comprehends." (Harari, 385)

If we take into account this statement we are yet to see what the future is going to bring into existence. With dataism the new religion and like Harari notes in his book, with human experience becoming more relevant only if it is shared online and with others, having your work online may become the only way for an author to reach his/her audience and partake his creation.

Let's take a look at some of the authors that are using social media platforms to showcase their works and explore how their work can fit into the criteria of a classic if at all.

Platform

Author Content and criteria they meet for a classic

Instagram

Robert Drake (@rmdrk)

A successful New York Times bestseller, his instagram account has 2. 4 million followers. His content is thought-provoking and insightful. Though he is a published author too, his online works are equally popular.

Paulo Coelho

(@paulocoelho)

Another popular published author whose novel The Alchemist is the third best-selling novel of all time. Already considered a classic, his Instagram feed which is full of inspiring quotes and Coelho in nature also has 1. 4 million followers.

@ttt_official

This is a platform with 1. 8 million followers. A quick look at its feed will reveal original stories and content by various contributors. From tiny tales, to imagery to stories in the form of text messages, this platform has it all. Some of the stories have gained immense popularity and could be considered classics in themselves.

@thescribbledstories Another popular handle with 3. 3 million followers. It also consists of original popular content.

Kash Bhattacharya

@budgettraveller Well-known for his travel writing, his instagram also boasts 34. 1k followers. His content on Instagram consists of beautiful pictures and

Twitter Fiction

Elliot Holt An award-winning author, through her work she has shown how twitter can be used to write great prose.

Craig Taylor A contributor to the Twitter fiction festival, he wrote a 140-character limit story.

Francesca Simon Same as above

Margaret Atwood The veteran writer has taken on the new platform with a storm to experiment in the new literary form.

Matt Stewart He wrote a whole novel on Twitter and then found a publisher for the same.

The above examples are just a few to showcase how established as well as new authors are experimenting with and utilizing the new platforms for their craft and gaining a readership. The fact that their stories do have a beginning, middle and end, a proper plot gives a new twist to the old 'classic. ' An author has to connect to the audience wherever they maybe, so if they are online and are accepting of the new formats and narratives, then there they will be.

1.5 CONCLUSION

We have seen in this chapter what the criteria of defining the classics are. It is observed that creativity assessment in language art writing is a big problem and it is more or less established over a period time through popularity in readership.

Regarding classics in digital era following is observed

In his lecture Eliot (1945) observed, "There is no classic in English". Mukherjee (2010) also writes that English is a living language with various vagaries and possibly the greatest capacity of changing yet remaining itself.

The classics are always a reflection of their times with an element of immortality. The works produced in current times reflect the socio-political and technological advancements of this epoch. The very art of composing has been transformed due to the new technologies and the author is not isolated from that.

As discussed above, a classic stimulates the reader and if the reader is to be found online on different platforms then that is where the writer will also be. Therefore, just as we are witnessing the evolution of a new language, maybe it is the time to see the evolution of the classics. After all eternal truths can be expressed in 280-characters and a determined fan of a work will find the published work online if he/she really wants to.

CHAPTER V

DUBIOUS AUTHENTICITY OF CROWD – SOURCED CREATION

Overview

Technological advancements and digital media have affected traditional gatekeeping contribution. Digital media platforms through Web 2. 0 technologies have made the traditional contribution of gatekeeper's non-existent. This chapter examines consequences and remedies for absence of traditional filters of traditional gate keeping.

1.1 Role of Gatekeepers in the Digital Age

A book is usually considered the brainchild of the author. However, "published books are almost always products of collaboration." (Rettberg, 187)

Of course there are books that are written by various authors but what we are looking here is at is the collaboration of editors, designers, publishers, and distributors to create the final product – the book. (Ibid). As Rettberg points out in his paper, not many people really pay attention to the people fulfilling these roles, in fact, many may not even be aware of their existence. Though this obvious exclusion is as much a need of the market as the emphasis given to the genius of the writer. Everything else takes a backseat. Be that as may be there are many writers who themselves acknowledge the work of leading editors who help them shape their book and its message. And where would graphic novels be or for that matter remembers the age old age – "never judge the book by its cover?" They are point to the crucial role designers play in helping sell books.

Let me now delve into the role of gatekeeper in more detail. The editor is one of the last people to go over a manuscript before it is ready for print. He or she will examine the document for inconsistencies in theme, style, and factual information. Permission is checked for copyright material, ensuring there will be no legal conflict. Grammar, spelling, and punctuation are also scanned again. The main purpose of the copy editor is to make sure the text that is used is clear, will maintain the interest of the reader, and maintain in-house style rules.

Editor examines the document for inconsistencies, unnecessary repetitions, factual information, whether permission has been obtained for copyright material, grammar, spelling, and presentation style. Intervention of the editor many times ensures that document will maintain the reader interest. He refines the text.

Authors have spent considerable hours in developing the stories. There basic essence of involvement is to expand an idea into creative writing. They are emotionally attached to their text. They may overlook the important requirements of manuscript ensured by editors.

Roger W. Sperry was awarded the Nobel Prize in Physiology or Medicine in 1981. The Prize motivation: "for his discoveries concerning the functional specialization of the cerebral hemispheres." Both human and animal brains have two halves with somewhat different functions. By the 1960s, he could reveal that the left hemisphere is more geared toward abstract and analytical thought, calculation, and linguistic ability, while the right hemisphere is more important for comprehending spatial patterns and complex sounds like music. (https://www. nobelprize. org/prizes/medicine/1981/sperry/facts/)

In short left brain is analytical and right brain is creative.

However, later research has shown that the brain is not nearly as neatly divided as this. The brain actually works best when both sides of the brain are engaged at the same time. https://hummingbirdlearning. com/use-your-brain-for-a-change/

Even though the Roger W. Spray research that left brain is analytical and right brain is creative is now debated by later research but the fact remains creativity and analytical aptitude are two different capabilities and skill set.

Creating a piece of creative writing is an act of creativity whereas editing that text is an act of analytical domain.

I will not like to call creativity as skill set as skill is something which can be acquired with practice. Whereas in my opinion is an aptitude with which a person is born with. It is in my view a part of a person's DNA. However, to be accomplished creative writer to create outstanding literature one has to polish this aptitude. While the skill as an editor can be acquired with practice.

So can an author be both Author as well as editor. Theoretically the answer is yes. But my experience both as a writer and professional editor is that it a tough call while editing your own manuscript. You tend to digress in to creative mode every time you make an effort to edit your own work. You have to make conscience effort to block your creative instinct to remain in editing mode. It requires lot of practice over and above practice required to acquire editing skill. The time required to hone the skill depends upon nature of guidance available, ability to acquire skill and natural talent.

However, my own experience and practice in the publishing industry suggestive of the fact that it requires second eye to iron out the deficiencies which editorial intervention intends to clear out. In fact, practice in industry is to have review by third eye as well-second eye being that of editor and third eye that of proof editor. First eye is of course that of an author. Writing and editing by gatekeepers are two different processes the collaboration which creates a final product.

. Never has this collaboration between authors and gatekeepers being more evident than in the world of electronic publishing and in a way to its extension – the social media platforms. It is only in this world that these background scorers get their fair amount of publicity. With the advent and rise of e-publishing, the self-publishing has taken on a life of its own. Though in today's times a number of well-known publishers and editors have launched services of apps that help an author to polish his/her book – in the absence of the cohesive world of traditional publishing, the author has to don these multiple hats himself to get his book out.

Same is the case of blogging platforms, where people writing blogs use the existing CMSs to write, insert media, choose font and layout and then publish their blog.

One more aspect which is very important is assessing the quality of manuscript in terms of it being potential to be classic. This shallwill be discussed later in the chapter.

1.2 Gatekeepers of quality

When we discuss issue of quality of manuscripts of creative writing, we can split the concept of quality into two levels.

At level 1 is the issue whether manuscript is well polished one meaning thereby as discussed above it has seen the intervention of gatekeeper for inconsistencies, unnecessary repetitions, factual information, whether permission has been obtained for copyright material, grammar, spelling, presentation style.

At level 2 Even if the manuscripts meets the requirement of level 1 whether it can be considered an outstanding piece of creative writing as discussed in chapter 4.

The interesting question that arises now in the context of social media platforms is that of editors. In this chapter we will attempt to see what impact do gatekeepers of quality – editors – have on creative writing and what happens when they are removed from the equation of publishing a piece of creative writing.

In academic writing, editors and publishers are called "gatekeepers" traditionally. This is because the editors are largely responsible for ensuring that only the best quality text or content is accepted or allowed to enter the hallowed portals of the publisher. The editors also thoroughly work through the text, reading it reviewing it first to see whether it is fit to be considered for publishing at all or not and then editing it. They ensure that the language is correct and grammatical inconsistencies are ironed out, apart from ensuring form, style, continuity and judgment, before the book can be published and released into the market.

In his paper "Gatekeeper as a metaphor and concept" Ikuyo Sato notes "It is widely acknowledged that book editors play a key role as intermediaries between the production and consumption of printed (and now, increasingly, electronic as well) cultural materials. Whether working chiefly in literary, journalistic, or scholarly fields, editors – especially those at prestigious publishing houses – are usually expected to winnow a vast number of potential manuscripts down to only a few so as to bring them and their authors to attention of the consuming public. By serving as gatekeepers who decide on what and whom should be let in, with the remainder kept out, editors sometimes play a considerable part in shaping not only the content and quality of specific books but also the overall configurations of various cultural fields."

Sato puts in perspective exactly the point that we have been discussing. However, in his essay he notes that the description of gatekeepers can be limiting since an editor's daily activities are much more than that. In our case, we expand the term gatekeepers from just acquiring and sifting manuscripts to also ensuring the sanctity of the manuscript once it is accepted for publishing. Sato also discusses the role of an editor more comprehensively by discussing the nine sub-roles of a scholarly editor as proposed by Sanford Thatcher (1994, 1999). They are – "hunter, selector, shaper, linker, stimulator, shepherd, promoter, ally and reticulator." (Sato, 46)

For the purposes of our research I am borrowing this concept for understanding the role that Gatekeepers play in maintaining quality and how it is relevant across genres.

It would be fair to say that a "classic" is as much a genius of the writer as the labour of love of the editor.

1.3 Social Media Platforms and Gatekeeping

We have discussed the dawn and development of social media platforms in the previous chapters. We also took a look at how new narrative styles have evolved due to these platforms and technological evolution in chapter 2 and 3. Apart from this we saw how English language has morphed due to the need of platforms and new age communication in chapter3.

If we research on the language and creative writing trends in Digital Revolution, we find that a number of linguists and grammar purists have raised concerns over the decline in the quality of English language as a result of social media.

The main aim of these platforms is to express, communicate instantly and connect with others. Over time they have transformed into platforms for budding authors and creators to showcase their talents.

As a result, anyone with an inclination can now become an author publishing their works online for others to consume and comment on. A fallout of this trend has been the English language. Not much attention is paid to the sentence structures, the syntax, correctness of words used. The only focus being to get out content fast. What is missing from this equation are editors. Most platforms do not have the option of an editor going through the posts before going "live" unless it is a digital marketing campaign where people actually take pains to ensure all this is correct.

Let's take a look at some examples:

1. Blogging platforms

Most blogging platforms whether it be Medium or WordPress have a content management Software (CMS) where the author can write their text, insert images or even a video in their content. They can then add trending hashtags to help drive traffic to their blogs. A content management system, often abbreviated as CMS, is software that helps users create, manage, and modify content on a website without the need for specialized technical knowledge.

But they do not have an option for an editor to got through the text and edit it. Of course, these days' apps like Grammarly are available for free and paid subscription to help correct any errors.

Nevertheless, anyone who has used these Apps would know that they are not 100% accurate. In the sense, one has to used their own judgment while incorporating the suggested changes especially in the free version and thus needs to be aware of the basic rules of grammar to choose the right option keeping in mind the context of the work and even style – something a "human" editor is trained for.

2. Twitter

We've discussed in detail the format of this platform in previous chapter. To reiterate, when someone posts a "tweet", the most they can choose the option of autocorrect which appears if they have downloaded and added Grammarly to their browser. Like in the example above, an intervention by a human editor can go a long way in preserving the sanctity of the text being written.

3. Facebook

Another popular social platform where people can write and post instantly.

Again there are no editorial interventions to help correct the language.

1.4 Collaborative work on the World Wide Web

One distinctive feature of World Wide Web is the collaboration it affords to creators of content. Rettberg in his essay explores the issue of what happens when collaborative work is edited or not. He observes that collaborative work almost always exclusively works on constraints if it has to be successful. These constraints are either explicitly agreed on by the creators or built into the system for that creates the work (Rettberg, Thomas&Page, 194). If collaborative web narratives that anyone can contribute to on the network are to be successful as stories then either a subset of contributors has to edit it or there has to be an inbuilt mechanism in the system creating it for the same.

While Rettberg raises an important point that explores our idea of managing content online he shares an example that shows that extensive regulation in the past- faced content consuming times like ours, can in fact be a failure.

Rettberg takes the example of Wikipedia where content is contributed by users and can be modified by any of the users. (Rettberg, Thomas&Page, 199). "Tim O' Reilly has described systems like Wikipedia as 'architectures of participation, ' systems in which 'a grassroots user base creates a self-regulating collaborative network (O'Reilly, 2004)" (Rettberg, Thomas&Page, 194).

What this indicates is that moving forward, one of the options open to us is to build self-regulating collaborative networks and trust the collective intelligence of the network to correct the content and check its veracity. Though this does not seem like an ideal solution it does seem to work as far as Wikipedia is concerned. However, even if the language is checked for structure and grammar, the fact check may not be relied on making it not a trustworthy source of content.

On the other hand, Nupedia, which was an ancestor in a way to Wikipedia and had failed as a platform, also indicates how over-regulation may not work in an online network. Nupedia wanted its content to be created and vetted by research scholars and in a way failed to trust the intelligence of the collective. As a result, it not only failed to take off, but by the time it shut down it was able to produce and publish only 24 articles which had been peer reviewed. ((Rettberg, Thomas&Page, 199).

1.5 Limitations of Apps for Gatekeeping on Narrative on digital platforms

While discussing gatekeeper for quality in para 5. 2 we have discussed two level of quality intervention by gatekeepers. At level 1 is the intervention to see whether manuscript is well polished. It has been discussed that there are apps like Grammar, available for free and paid subscription to help correct any errors. Of course such apps also have limitations.

At other level at level 2 is even if the manuscripts meets the requirement of level 1 whether it can be considered an outstanding piece of creative writing This intervention of gatekeeping especially enforced at prestigious publishing houses – are usually expected to winnow a vast number of potential manuscripts down to only a few so as to bring them and their authors to attention of the consuming public.

In chapter 4 criteria which define an outstanding piece of creative writing have been identified. I shall like done down the adjective "outstanding" for our purpose to the one which will be "popular" among readers or the one reader will like to read. Like at least there are apps to for level-1 gatekeeping efforts, is it possible have to digital intervention to perform Level 2 quality intervention. It has been established from criteria defined in chapter 4 for outstanding creative writing that that if we want to evaluate piece of creative writing when it is created as to whether it is outstanding piece of literature it is no easy task. The aspect of assessment of creativity seems to be a problematic to the extent that whether creative writing can be assessed is a big question mark. One important reason for this is that such evaluation falls in the realms of emotions. How does the creative work appeals to the feelings of reader? Such evaluation is not analytical. An gatekeeper can make this evaluation though evaluation can differ from person to person. But it is, at the present level of digital evaluation, is not possible to digitize Even advancement in artificial intelligence have yet to progress in field of emotional evaluation.

1.6 Conclusion

In the second chapter we took a detailed look at the new kinds of narratives that technical advancement has allowed.

From hybrid texts to fan pages to YouTube channel to people responding to posts – everything now comes under the purview of Creative Writing.

Though we take a look above at how editors can improve the quality of content online, it is also a fact that they can delay the process of posting and thus defeat the whole idea of writing on social media.

Alternatively, in the absence of editors there is a marked decrease in the quality of creative writing available online. Some find the content that the new age authors churn out as replete with errors and violating the laws of grammar, thus bringing about a death of the correct language.

After all, isn't it true, that nobody likes to read a Facebook post or even a text message that is written in incorrectEnglish?

1.7 Framework the need of the hour

What is needed now is a hybrid model wherein an editorial framework can help correct the inconsistencies before content is published online. As we saw above, this can either be achieved through peer review or edited by users or other collaborators on the platform as seen in the case of Wikipedia, which empowers each individual user to act on behalf of the collective and clearly segregates power among them (Rettberg, Thomas&Page, 200). Another example of how the collaborators community can be harnessed to edit text is that of fanfiction review culture. In case of fanfiction sites there are "built-in mechanisms facilitating systematic and ongoing reviews that help to generate a 'review culture' among fans, whereby the roles of authors and readers become virtually interchangeable (Chatelain 2002)." (Thomas, Thomas&Page, 209). The review process and social interaction on such sites allows some kind of aesthetic critique of the stories is offered and departure from the canon is pointed out (Thomas, Thomas&Page, 209). The authors on such sites can also take the assistance of Betareaders who are basically experienced writers and often the admins of such sites (Thomas, Thomas&Page, 209). They can offer a range of advice from correcting spellings to punctuation to plot and character construction. Thomas observes that "while Betareaders fulfill an editorial role, and usually have to be selected and trained to do so, anybody registered on the sites can post reviews of published stories" (Thomas, Thomas&Page, 209).

This is another way in which editorial input before a text is published can be utilized, however, the argument against this remains the same. How do we ensure that editorial input can be given for posts being done in realtime?

This can also be achieved either through human intervention or AI- based apps that improve performance over time, based on the data fed in them, so that we can see English restored to its proper glory.

Conversely, we can accept the new changes occurring in the Language as the next step in evolution of English and give ourselves upto it. Or as Victor Gollancz a famous publisher had famously rejected the role of editors. He firmly believed that it was the publisher's duty to tell the author what he thought but it was entirely upto the latter to accept this judgment and implement it. Rick Gokeski in his article on "The importance of good editing" in the New York Times, observes that though Gollancz was aware of the importance of good editing he was worried that all books worked on by an inhouse editor in a publishing house could turn it formulaic.

CHAPTER VI

CONCLUSION

In an article in the Forbes magazine, reporter Bernard Marr observes that how many notable organizations are now using AI to generate content.

This could be the future of Creative Writing. Over the last few pages and chapters we saw how Creative Writing has journeyed over the ages, and how it almost became fossilized in classrooms of English Departments. However, with the technological advancements of the last few years, writers have had at their disposal tools and technologies that allowed them to experiment with their craft. From the earliest Hypertext novels to e-publishing to social media, the plethora of platforms and formats available to a creative writer is manifold.

What changed the game was the advent of the World Wide Web. With its democratic nature, ability to connect people instantly and various content communities where people could express and publish instantly, we saw a glut of self-proclaimed authors flooding the world.

Unfortunately, though now people were free of the limitations of publishers, not all content available online could be said to be of a good standard.

Social Media platforms and creative writing

Moving on to specifically the social media platforms, there are as many formats as there are platforms. Authors are now creating fiction on Twitter with 280 characters, are writing stories that are a mix of images, animation, music and hashtags on Instagram, or are blogging.

Another change that social media has brought about is that it has transformed English language completely. From abbreviations to slang to even emojis, people are using all kinds of variations to express themselves. And it has come into everyday parlance. However, what are the limitations and positives of this evolution?

Positives

The World Wide Web is a democratic setup, and has given an opportunity for authors to directly engage and reach their audience without any middlemen such as publishers. They are using these platforms to gain followers and then introduce them to their writing or are even writing for these platforms.

From cellphone novels to twitter fiction to Insta stories and reels to Facebook posts – people are using new formats to tell a story.

The language has also become democratized. We have broken the silos of Eastern/Anglo-Indian/Western Literature to become Twitter or Insta story instead.

The language is also no longer British English or American English but just the authors words. However, since American English is simpler in its rules, it is gaining popularity which could be a good trend or result in another language autocracy replacing British English. Chances of that happening are less though.

Limitations

The trend is not all positive. With the glut of authors and over information in the market, its easy to get lost in bad content. Gatekeeping which ensured the quality of writing is now diluted and needs to be brought back in some form.

Language itself is losing its sanctity and we need to recognize the same. At the same time creative writing on social media is yet to come up with new terminologies to describe the new formats being created instead of using existing terminologies which are limited in their being originating from print which is an older form.

Conclusion

We need to redefine Creative Writing and accept that it is changed beyond recognition. With the rise of digital humanities, its time we accept Creative Writing needs a new definition and terminology in the new age.

Also, since English language has always evolved over the years, and today's generation reads in this language, this new form may need to be accepted as is. If Bob Dylan can win a Nobel Prize for Literature for songs then who is to say the future Nobel winner is not tweeting his story right now?

At the same time, since we are in a transitional period, we need to encourage a new framework of Gatekeeping in the digital age, wither through AI or Peer Review to maintain speed and at the same time bring about quality.

This area of research is still evolving and there is a lot to still explore. I hope this paper raises some questions and answers some doubts and gives a platform to future researchers to take it forward.

References

- AndrewsKimberly (2009) A House Divided: On the Future of Creative Writing, *College English* Vol. 71, No. 3, Jan., 2009 Published by: National Council of Teachers of English.
- Baron Carole (2010) Is It the Thought That Counts? Or Is It the Book? HUFFPOST Updated May 25, 2011 Retrieved 3rd January 2021. https://www. huffpost.com/entry/is-it-the-thought-that-co_b_35993
- Barth, Rodney J. & Thom Swiss, (1976), "The Impact of Television on Reading," *The Reading Teacher*, Vol.30, No.2 (November, 1976), 236–239.
- Barth, Rodney J. & Thom Swiss. (1976) The Impact of Television on Reading; *The Reading Teacher*, Vol. 30, No. 2, 236–239.
- BartkyElliot(1992) The Review of Politics,, Vol. 54, No. 4, Special Sesquicentennial Issue (Autumn, 1992), pp. 589-619.
- Coulmas Florian (2005) "Changing Language Regimes in Globalizing Environments,", *International Journal of the Sociology of Language,* Vol. 175–176, Issue 175-176 (October, 2005), pp. 3–15.
- Coulmas, F. (2005). Changing Language Regimes in Globalizing Environments; *International Journal of the Sociology of Language,* Vol. 175–176, Issue 175-176, pp. 3–15.
- Dean Jodi, (2003): Why the Net Is not a Public Sphere, *Constellations* Volume 10, no. 1 (2003): 102.
- Dexter, Lewis A. "Books: The Culture and Commerce of Publishing. By Lewis A. Coser, Charles Kadushin, and Walter W. Powell. (New York: Basic Books, 1982. Pp. Xiii 411. $19. 00.)." American Political Science Review, vol. 76, no. 4, 1982, pp. 897–898., doi:10.1017/S000305540018983X.
- Epstein Jason (2010) Publishing: The Revolutionary Future *The New York Review of Books* March 11, 2010 issue https://www.nybooks.com/articles/2010/03/11/publishing-the-revolutionary-future/
- Garcia Landa, Jose Angel, (1986) *Plato's Poetics. inHypercritica: A Hypertextual History of Literary Criticism*. Available at SSRN: https://ssrn.com/abstract=2414535or http://dx.doi.org/10.2139/ssrn.2414535.

- Gekoski Rick (2012) The importance of good editing The Guardian Thu 14 Jun 2012 https://www.theguardian.com/books/2012/jun/14/importance-good-book-editing.
- Gharbawi, Alaa, Revolution of the Internet, https://sites.cs.ucsb.edu/~almeroth/classes/F04. 176A/homework1_good_papers/Alaa- Gharbawi. html. Accessed on October 1, 2020.
- Harper Graeme (2014) The *Future for Creative Writing*, John Wiley & Sons, Incorporated, 2014.
- Harper, G. (2014) *The Future of Creative Writing*; John Wiley & Sons, Inc.
- Hayles, N. Katherine(2002) *Writing Machines*Mediaworks Pamphlets
- Historyextra. com. *'Green-eyed monster' and 'stiff upper lip': the evolution of the English language* 'The official website for BBC History MagazineAccessed on October 2, 2020. https://www. historyextra. com/period/norman/how-english-language-evolved-inkhorn-controversy-shakespeare-phrases-in-use-today-who-invented-english/
- Horobin, S. (2018) *The English Language: A Very Short Introduction*; Oxford University Press.
- Internet Revolution." U*X*L Encyclopedia of U. S. History.. Encyclopedia. com. Updated 12 Jan. 2021 Accessed on January 30 2021. <https://www.encyclopedia.com>.
- James Fyfe, Rita James Simon Editors as Gatekeepers - Getting Published in the Social Sciences, Rowman& Littlefield, 1994.
- Kinds Of Writing: Student Conceptions Of Academic And Creative Forms Of Writing Development, L. Hutton, & G. Gibson, In Gere A. (Ed.), Developing Writers in Higher Education: A Longitudinal Study (pp. 89-112), Ann Arbor: University of Michigan Press. Retrieved from http://www.jstor.org/stable/j.ctvdjrpt3. 9. Accessed on 12 July 2019.
- Koehler Coulmas Adam (2013) Digitizing Craft: Creative Writing Studies and New Media: A Proposal, *College English* 75, no. 4 (2013): 379-97.
- Koehler, A. (2013) Digitizing Craft: Creative Writing Studies and New Media: A Proposal; *College English* 75, no. 4, pp. 379-97. www.jstor.org/stable/24238180. Accessed 21 September 2020.
- Koehler, Adam. (2013) "Digitizing Craft: Creative Writing Studies and New Media: A Proposal." *College English, vol. 75, no. 4, 2013,* pp. 379–397. JSTOR, www.jstor.org/stable/24238180. Accessed 21 Sept. 2020. Copy.
- Maxwell Perkins. Britannica, The Editors of Encyclopaedia Britannica, 16 Sep. 2020, Accessed 26 January 2021. https://www.britannica.com/biography/Maxwell-Perkins.

- McCrum Robert (2010) Publishing will always need its gatekeepers The Guardian 1 Mar 2010. https://www.nybooks.com/articles/2010/03/11/publishing-the-revolutionary-future/
- MUKHERJEE, A. (2010). "What Is a Classic?" International Literary Criticism and the Classic Question. *PMLA,* 125(4), 1026-1042. Retrieved October 8, 2020, from http://www. jstor. org/stable/41058302
- Murray J. (2017) Hamlet on the Holodeck – The Future of Narrative Cyberspace. The Free Press.
- Myers, D. G(1993) The Rise of Creative Writing. *Journal of the History of Ideas* Vol. 54, No. 2, Apr., 1993 Published By: University of Pennsylvania Press
- *New England Review (1990-)*Vol. 23, No. 3 (Summer, 2002), pp. 100-110 (11 pages)Published by: Middlebury College Publicationshttps://www-jstor-org. library. britishcouncil. org. in:4443/stable/40244153on 6 april 2020
- Novak, K. &Smailovic, Jasmina&Sluban, Borut&Mozetic, Igor. (2015). Sentiment of Emojis. PloS one. 10. 10. 1371/journal. pone. 0144296. https://www. researchgate. net/publication/282270290_Sentiment_of_Emojis/citation/do wnload. Accessed on October 4, 2020.
- O'Regan G. (2008) The Internet Revolution. In: O'Regan G. (eds) *A Brief History of Computing. Springer, London.* https://doi. org/10. 1007/978-1-84800-084-1_6Accessed on October 1, 2020
- Page, Ruth, Bronwen Thomas (2011) New *Narratives: Stories and Storytelling in the Digital Age* (Frontiers of Narrative) University of Nebraska Press.
- Parsons P. Getting Published: The Acquisition Process at University Presses (University of Tennessee Press), 1989.
- Powell W. Getting into Print: The Decision-Making Process in Scholarly Publishing (U. of Chicago Press, 1985)
- PRESS ASSOCIATION (1 May 2015) Generational language gap 'seismic' *Mail Online* https://www.dailymail.co.uk/wires/pa/article-3063505/Generational-language-gap-seismic.html. Accessed on October 1, 2020.
- Roy, Dhananjay (2012) "Cell Phone Novel – A New Genre of Literature," *Language in India,* Vol. 12, No. 3 (March, 2012), p. 81.
- Rudin Michael (2011) From Hemingway to Twitterature: The Short and Shorter of It *The Journal of Electronic Publishing (JEP)* Volume 14, Issue 2, Fall 2011 https://quod.lib.umich.edu/j/jep/3336451.0014.213?view=text;rgn=main.
- Rudin Michael (Fall 2011) From Hemingway to Twitterature: The Short and Shorter of It Journal of electronic publishing Volume 14, Issue 2, Fall 2011https://quod.lib.umich.edu/j/jep/3336451.0014.213?view=text;rgn=main.

- Sato, I. (2012). "GATEKEEPER" AS A METAPHOR AND CONCEPT. Hitotsubashi Journal of Commerce and Management, 46(1 (46)), 41-50. Retrieved October 1, 2020, from http://www.jstor.org/stable/43295039
- Schwab, Ing. Klaus. (2017). *The Fourth Industrial Revolution;* Penguin Books Ltd. Kindle Edition, p. 14.
- Sharaqi Laila Al (August 2016) Twitter Fiction: A New Creative Literary Landscape Advances in Language and Literary Studies Australian International Academic Centre, Australia Vol. 7 No. 4; August 2016 https://files.eric.ed.gov/fulltext/EJ1127321.pdf
- Sutherland, John. 'The Samsung Galaxy S6 Evolution of Text.' https://www.telegraph.co.uk/news/newstopics/howaboutthat/11574196/new-forms-of-social-media-terms-which-parents-do-not-understand.html. Accessed on October 1, 2020.
- Taylor Astra (2014) *The People's Platform: Taking Back Power and Culture in the Digital Age,* (New York: Metropolitan Books, 2014), p. 17.
- Thatcher S. Listbuilding at University Press. In Rita Simon & James Fyfe eds. 1994. Editors as Gatekeepers. Lanham, ML:Rowman and Littlefield.
- The Future of NLG March 30, 2019 https://www.agrudtech.com/the-future-of-nlg/. Accessed on September 29, 2020.
- The New Partridge Dictionary of Slang and Unconventional English. (2015.) Dalzell T., Victor T. (eds.), Routledge, 2nd edn., 2015.
- Vaidhyanathan Siva, (2011) *The Googlization of Everything: (And Why We Should Worry)*, (Berkeley and Los Angeles: Univ. of California Press, 2011).
- World Economic Forum Fourth Industrial Revolutionhttps://www.weforum.org/focus/fourth-industrial-revolution. Accessed on October 1, 2020.

www.ingramcontent.com/pod-product-compliance
Ingram Content Group UK Ltd.
Pitfield, Milton Keynes, MK11 3LW, UK
UKHW061828190726
13853UKWH00009B/2496